Managing Your
Boss and Colleagues

Managing Your
Boss and
Colleagues

*Manage your working relationships
and achieve your business goals*

STEVE GRAVETT

How To Books

Published by How To Books Ltd,
3 Newtec Place, Magdalen Road,
Oxford OX4 1RE, United Kingdom.
Tel: (01865) 793806. Fax: (01865) 248780.
email: info@howtobooks.co.uk
http://www.howtobooks.co.uk

British Library Cataloguing in Publication Data.
A catalogue record for this book is available from
the British Library.

Cover design by Shireen Nathoo Design
Cover image by PhotoDisc

Produced for How To Books by Deer Park Productions
Edited by Diana Brueton
Typeset by Kestrel Data, Exeter
Printed and bound by Cromwell Press, Trowbridge, Wiltshire

NOTE: The material contained in this book is set out in good
faith for general guidance and no liability can be accepted
for loss or expense incurred as a result of relying in particular
circumstances on statements made in the book. The laws and
regulations are complex and liable to change, and readers should
check the current position with the relevant authorities before
making personal arrangements.

Contents

List of Illustrations

Preface

It's one thing to know all about the latest management theories but quite another to be able to put the theory into practice. In the real world, people in the workplace do not behave in textbook fashion. Your boss and colleagues are human beings with their own mixture of strengths and weaknesses. They may even have serious shortcomings which make life at work intolerable.

This user-friendly book is written for everyone who goes out to work, and is seeking a practical guide with a down-to-earth approach to relationship issues at the workplace. It offers refreshing insights and helpful advice designed to enable you to keep the appropriate level of control over your workplace colleagues.

You can learn how to analyse your boss and compensate for any weaknesses you identify. Managing relationships with colleagues and becoming an effective team player is challenging. It is possible for you to develop effective strategies that maximise your inter-personal skills, develop your potential and help to enhance your career prospects.

One boss, Beryl, deserves a special mention. So do our three children, Jonathan, Jay and Faye who feature in the fictional case studies.

Steve Gravett

1

Managing Yourself

ANALYSING YOUR NEEDS

The alarm clock rings. It's Monday morning. You bound out of bed full of enthusiasm. It's time to get up and go to work. Does that sound like you?

Why do you go to work? Is it purely for the money? Getting a regular wage packet or salary cheque is important and the main driving force for most people. It means you can afford to live somewhere decent, drive a car, have a good time at the weekends and have an annual holiday.

It is possible you also enjoy working as part of a team, achieving something, or doing something creative. If you are a manager work meets your need to be in control, gives you status, power and influence. All these reasons are perfectly legitimate as they satisfy the need for self-esteem.

The hierarchy of needs

Many psychologists have tried to explain what motivates people. The most well known theory, the **hierarchy of needs**, was devised by Abraham Maslow. He believes we all have 'basic primary needs' which have to be met before you can move on to addressing what he calls 'higher level needs'. Maslow identified five levels of needs in ascending order of priority:

1. Basic needs
Food to prevent hunger, and clothing to keep out the cold.

2. Safety and security
Somewhere to live where you feel safe and secure.

3. Social needs
Meeting other people to share interests and make friends.

4. Self-esteem needs
The need for praise and recognition.

5. Self-actualisation needs
The need to achieve goals and fulfil your potential.

Feeling valued at work

Fredrick Herzberg identified two main reasons why people feel valued at work, which he describes as **motivators** and **hygiene factors**.

Things that contribute to the process of motivating people include:

- having a sense of achievement

- being appreciated and praised

- having responsibility

- doing an interesting job

- having promotion prospects.

Whilst hygiene factors do not appear to directly contribute to increased productivity, they are issues that affect how people feel about their place of work and role within the company. Anything that makes people feel more content at work is likely to contribute to increased productivity. These hygiene factors can include:

- the wages or level of salary you receive

- a pleasant working environment

- working for a company that does not exploit its employees

- working with friendly colleagues

- having a positive relationship with your boss.

Knowing what motivates you

Human behaviourists appreciate we all have a hidden agenda at work, namely to satisfy our own needs. Being happy and successful at work involves being able to identify what motivates you. Ask yourself:

- Do you need the approval of others?

- Do you have to be in control and be able to exercise power?

- Do you get a buzz from meeting deadlines or achieving targets?

If you do not feel fully satisfied at work, try to identify which of your needs are not being met.

UNDERSTANDING YOUR STRENGTHS

A positive attitude, self-confidence, a range of marketable skills and an agreeable personality are qualities and skills every employer is clamouring for.

Take a realistic look at your strengths (and weaknesses) and assess your market value with this skills audit.

List your skills and personal qualities under the following headings:

- Skills and qualifications

- Degree of motivation

- Working with others

- Professional strengths

- Problem-solving ability.

Skills and qualifications

Write down all your educational qualifications and list any professional qualifications you have gained. Don't forget to include any other formal training you have completed, and record all the courses you have attended. Finally, identify all those skills you have developed through experience.

Degree of motivation

Examine how highly motivated you are by asking yourself:

- Are you flexible?

- Are you prepared to do menial tasks and prove yourself?

- Are you willing to undertake further training?

- Can you work under pressure and meet deadlines?

- Are you resilient and able to cope with stress?

- Do you persevere when the going gets tough?

Working with others
You need to work harmoniously with others. Assess your ability to do so by answering these questions honestly:

- Can you get on with most people?

- Are you tolerant of others' shortcomings?

- Do you like handling responsibility?

- Can you work without supervision?

- Are you able to use your initiative?

- Is problem-solving something you enjoy?

- Do you mind being told what to do?

- Can you follow instructions?

- Do you cope with criticism without sulking or becoming hostile?

Professional strengths
Identify your strong points and list them under the following headings:

Personal qualities
- drive

- enthusiasm

- energy levels

- determination.

Character traits
- reliability

- thoroughness

- dedication

- integrity.

Essential skills
- communication skills (written and oral)

- analytical skills
- listening skills
- positive attitude.

Achievements
Think about any positive things you have contributed to the company. Compile a list of the ideas you have contributed, and any improvements you have made to:
(a) procedures
(b) systems
(c) quality control
(d) service delivery
(e) gaining good publicity.

Business acumen
Identify any projects or measures you have been involved in which have contributed to:
(a) improving efficiency
(b) increasing productivity
(c) generating new business
(d) adding to the profitability of the business.

Problem-solving ability

The most important skill you need is the ability to solve problems. This quality makes you valuable to an employer.

Visualise yourself as a person who sees every problem as a challenge to be overcome. Problem-solvers are always in demand. Their innovative approach, fresh ideas and lateral thinking skills can make all the difference. It's a fine line between success and failure, being profitable and making a loss. Remember everyone loves a winner.

KNOWING YOURSELF

Human behaviourists have been able to identify four distinct personality types:

- The **extrovert** is an outgoing, sociable type.
- The **introvert** is a reserved, quiet person.

- The **stable individual** is a calm, even-tempered person.

- The **unstable person** is an anxious, moody, temperamental individual.

Many people combine two of these personality traits so it is possible to also be:

- A **stable introvert**: shy, thoughtful, introspective and reserved.

- An **unstable introvert**: anxious, quiet, withdrawn and uncommunicative.

- A **stable extrovert**: confident, outgoing, talkative and relaxed.

- An **unstable extrovert**: moody, forceful, disruptive and easily bored.

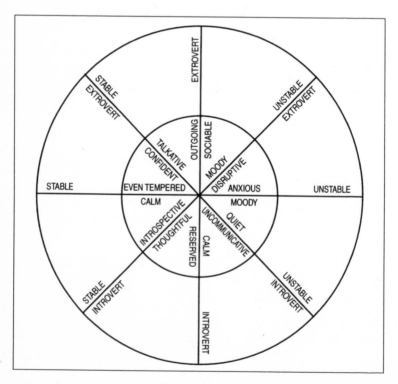

Fig. 1. The personality wheel.

Personality tests are widely used as a tool to recruit staff in commerce. However, there is no magic formula for establishing who is the best person for a particular job. Personality testing can be helpful in the process of seeking the right blend of personalities within a team. An effective team can be built by selecting people who complement each other, which is clearly beneficial to a company striving to increase productivity.

The personality wheel

The personality wheel (see Figure 1) allows you to pinpoint your main individual personality characteristics and identify your personality type. It also enables you to see which personalities complement each other and recognise how you could experience a personality clash.

HAVING A POSITIVE APPROACH

There is a fine dividing line between successful people and those living mundane, unfulfilling lives. Anyone who lacks self-confidence, has a low level of self-esteem, or entertains negative thoughts about their abilities, has programmed themselves for failure.

Learning to develop your charisma and become an inspirational leader takes energy and commitment. Successful people are self-confident, assertive, attractive, fun to be with, and influence others because they have developed an approach that harnesses the power of positive thinking.

Thinking positively

The keys to developing a positive approach are:

- self-belief
- valuing your uniqueness
- being self-reliant
- acting confidently
- learning to like yourself
- appreciating your good qualities
- not thinking negatively

- developing healthy thought patterns
- taking care of yourself
- living healthily
- relaxing and having fun
- smiling and enjoying life
- being open, receptive and approachable
- praising the achievements of others
- recognising your own achievements by rewarding yourself
- recognising and developing your talents
- remembering **you are a winner**.

Projecting yourself
The art of projecting the right image involves role play. Learning your part in the scheme of things means living the part convincingly. This can be achieved by visualising how you wish to be seen by others, then learning to play that role and living up to their expectations.

The essential ingredients for projecting yourself successfully are to:

- project energy and vitality
- enjoy your work
- think and act positively
- believe you are successful and part of a winning team
- make yourself attractive by taking care about your appearance and personal hygiene
- laugh at your own shortcomings, and appear not to take yourself too seriously.

Taking control
Although you cannot change your basic personality, you can learn to recognise, cultivate and use your existing talents.

Time is another constraint and limiting factor. Learn to treat time as another scarce resource. It ebbs away if it is not used properly.

To take control of your life you have to:

- take responsibility for the way you feel
- exercise self-discipline and control negative feelings
- be enthusiastic and believe in what you are doing
- always be positive.

Achieving positive outcomes

The benefits of taking control are that you:

- experience reduced stress levels
- have enhanced job satisfaction
- know the satisfaction of achieving your goals
- fulfil your potential
- maximise your value to the business.

BEHAVING PROFESSIONALLY

Although self-knowledge is important, its value is diminished if you do not apply these insights at work. The expected outcome from learning to manage yourself effectively should be a significant qualitative improvement in your performance.

A professional person is someone who has received specialist training and undertakes work that requires particular knowledge or expertise. **Professionalism** is demonstrated when the work produced reflects a combination of high standards and skill.

Someone who is described as a **dedicated professional** has excellent interpersonal skills and the ability to work harmoniously with their managers, colleagues and customers.

- Behaving professionally means always maintaining high standards.

Professional bodies set standards they expect their members to maintain. The Charter Marks Scheme, and the Investors in People initiative, were introduced to encourage organisations and individuals to achieve high professional standards.

Devising a personal charter

Devise a personal charter which reflects your values and standards. It should cover the following headings:

My treatment of others
- Am I available and acessible to colleagues?
- Do I listen to the concerns and frustrations of others?
- Are my relationships with others supportive and non-judgemental?
- Am I approachable, warm and friendly?

My appreciation of others
- Do I praise the achievements of others with enthusiasm?
- Am I receptive to ideas and suggestions?
- Can I accept criticism, and criticise others constructively?
- Do I practise open communication, keeping others aware of relevant matters, particularly issues that affect them?
- Am I understanding, objective and do I exercise self-control when things go wrong?

My commitment to others
- Do I consult others about how to improve their working conditions?
- Am I helping others to develop their potential?
- Does my style of leadership make others feel secure and perform to the best of their ability?
- Do I promote equal opportunities and respect the rights of minorities?
- Have I eliminated all forms of harassment from the workplace?

IMPROVING YOUR SKILLS

Any strategy for improving your skills will involve an ongoing commitment and include the regular review of your training needs. Ideally this should be a process which is owned by your employer, who sees the value of developing your full potential as beneficial to the company.

Acquired prior learning

Do not underestimate the skills you have already acquired. At school you acquired essential core skills, such as literacy, numeracy and the ability to use information technology. These may have been augmented by attending college or university to gain a vocational skill or a professional qualification. Other job-specific skills, gained through experience, may only apply to a particular employer such as operating their financial accounting systems.

Transferable skills

Anyone working for a number of years will have learnt a number of generic professional skills: participating in and chairing meetings; writing reports, proposals and business letters; and a range of interpersonal skills. Finally, there are individual, specific skills which include your positive attitude, high level of motivation, team leadership skills and political awareness.

Conducting a skills audit

The first priority is to conduct a **skills audit**. The annual staff appraisal report can be a helpful tool in identifying skill deficiencies as perceived by your line manager. You may discover they have given scant regard to your professional development prior to you raising the matter. Few managers give any thought to how to develop their own skills, so don't be surprised if for once they are lost for words about how to develop yours.

Self-improvement strategies

If you are a well motivated individual there is enormous scope to develop your skills and broaden your knowledge base:

- joining a professional association

- subscribing to a relevant magazine or trade journal

- purchasing books by leading exponents in your field

- joining the local public library and using the full range of information services and resources available

- using the Internet to keep abreast of latest developments

- undertaking a course of further study.

Further training

There are several ways to obtain further training. Your local College of Further Education, Job Centre, or Training Enterprise

Council can all offer advice. Colleges and universities offer a wide range of courses that lead to:

- accredited trade training
- professional qualifications
- management training leading to a recognised qualification.

Your employer may be willing to invest in your future by seconding you for a recognised course of study. Alternatively, distance learning is an option where you undertake a relevant correspondence course, or study with the Open University.

Being visible

Take every opportunity to attend courses provided by your employer, including:

- conferences, seminars and workshops
- representing the company at trade fairs and exhibitions
- participating in relevant working groups
- networking at meetings and getting yourself known.

Exploring other possibilities

Other possibilities worth exploring to gain knowledge, skills and wider experience include:

- job exchanges/swops
- a sideways or cross-hierarchy move
- a change in your functional responsibilities
- finding a suitable person to act as your mentor, to guide your professional development.

KNOWING YOUR FUTURE VALUE TO THE BUSINESS

It is important to be realistic about your worth to your employer. Everyone can be replaced, and once you've left you are soon forgotten. Be realistic. If you believe you are indispensable, sooner or later you will receive a rude awakening. Assess your value to the business by identifying:

- your direct contribution, eg the volume of sales you personally generate;
- the added value you contribute to the work of others, eg the volume of sales your area team generate under your leadership due to your skills at motivating and organising them.

Your value to the business is also related to the amount of power you wield. This can take several forms and is not restricted to your formal role and position in the organisation or outlined in your job description.

Assessing forms of power

Expertise
Your knowledge of the company's culture, the level of skills and competencies you have acquired, your training and professional qualifications.

Authority
Your ability to influence colleagues and customers, the leadership qualities you display, your personal popularity with colleagues and those you lead.

Control of resourses
The extent of budgetary control devolved to you, your ability to allocate work and popular tasks, the discretion you exercise over others' earning power and bonuses, your ability to fire and hire and promote staff.

Derived influence
Holding a position of responsibility in a trade union, having specialised knowledge (eg computer systems), access to confidential personnel information, knowledge about the future plans of the business, personal relationships with influential people.

Taking stock

Take your company's organisational chart and make a list of who controls resources and influences activities that affect you. Identify those individuals in the organisation who have the ability to obstruct or help you to achieve your objectives.

Assess each individual's source of authority and power and ask yourself:

- Are some of your frustrations at work caused by having insufficient power and influence?

- Is there any scope to alter the balance of power in your favour?

- Can you network more effectively and exercise greater influence?

- Do you need to devise a strategy which broadens your power base?

CREATING THE RIGHT IMAGE

Creating an image of yourself as a successful, dynamic leader needs to be carefully cultivated. Compile a professional portfolio with the following marketable assets:

- relevant formal qualifications

- a range of skills and competencies

- well-developed interpersonal skills

- personal qualities like honesty, reliability, integrity and demonstrable self-awareness

- evidence of professional achievement and credibility

- a good reputation.

An impressive list of professional skills is of limited value if you fail to understand how to relate meaningfully to others at work.

Concentrate on creating a positive first impression. It's much easier to build on a firm foundation than recover from a rocky start, because people quickly form impressions and voice their opinions to colleagues.

The following skills are absolutely essential for success:

- displaying appropriate body language, eg a firm handshake

- a smart and tidy appearance

- a friendly smile

- making good eye contact, as this helps to
  - build rapport
  - demonstrate confidence
  - establish trust
  - convey you are interested in what the other person has to say.

The career success formula

A survey titled *A Question of Balance?* was produced by Karen Charlesworth who questioned 2,500 managers, all members of the Institute of Management. It examined managers' changing professional and personal roles, and identified four important factors which make the difference between enjoying career success and failure. These factors can be summarised in the DISC approach:

- **D**etermination

- **I**nterpersonal skills

- **S**kills (relevant to the business)

- **C**ontacts.

Creating a recipe for success

The recipe for personal success is to possess the following important ingredients:

- a positive attitude

- the ability to be assertive

- self-confidence in your own abilities

- being recognised as an expert in your chosen specialism.

SELF-APPRAISAL

Marketing yourself to prospective employers, or ensuring your contribution is valued by your existing boss, means being aware of your strengths and weaknesses.

Employers like proactive, self-reliant people who have excellent inter-personnal skills, are highly motivated, flexible and get things done to a high standard within the time constraints.

Assessing how you are shaping up
Evaluate yourself and your skills with this questionnaire.

	Yes	No	Sometimes
Are you proactive or reactive?			
(a) You like introducing new initiatives.			
(b) 'If it ain't bust don't fix it!' is your motto.			
(c) 'Keep one step ahead of the others' is your attitude.			
(d) You can accept advice and guidance positively.			
Are you confident or modest?			
(a) You are always able to meet deadlines.			
(b) You like to tell others about your achievements.			
(c) You do not consider yourself to be boastful.			
(d) Receiving praise makes you feel embarrassed.			
Is your managerial style autocratic or democratic?			
(a) It is important to be in control and tell others what to do.			
(b) You feel it is important to reach a consensus.			
(c) Consultation is valuable but the final decision rests with you.			
(d) You resent being told what to do.			

	Yes	No	Sometimes

Is your approach rigid or flexible?
(a) You believe traditional ways have much to commend them.
(b) You always embrace changes positively.
(c) You get irritated when you hear others harp back to the 'good old days'.
(d) You would welcome an increase in your current responsibilties.

Are you task-orientated or a motivator?
(a) It is important to maintain a balance between achieving deadlines and keeping everyone happy.
(b) Targets must be met whatever the cost.
(c) You encourage staff to use their initiative.
(d) How others are feeling matters more than getting the job done on time.

Are you a risk-taker or indecisive?
(a) You find it difficult to make decisions.
(b) You are concerned that something may go wrong and you will receive the blame.
(c) You refer problems to someone else if you can.
(d) You make the decisions which make you popular.

Are you ambitious or do you have low self-esteem?
(a) There is no such thing as a problem, only a challenge.

	Yes	No	Sometimes
(b) You are keen to demonstrate your ability.			
(c) You can achieve anything if you apply yourself.			
(d) Your career comes before everything else.			

How did you score?

Proactive/reactive?

(a) Yes 3	(b) Yes 2	(c) Yes 3	(d) Yes 3
No 1	No 3	No 1	No 1
Sometimes 2	Sometimes 3	Sometimes 2	Sometimes 2

Confidence/modesty?

(a) Yes 3	(b) Yes 2	(c) Yes 3	(d) Yes 1
No 1	No 1	No 1	No 3
Sometimes 2	Sometimes 3	Sometimes 2	Sometimes 2

Autocratic/democratic?

(a) Yes 1	(b) Yes 3	(c) Yes 3	(d) Yes 1
No 3	No 1	No 1	No 3
Sometimes 2	Sometimes 2	Sometimes 2	Sometimes 2

Rigidity/flexibility?

(a) Yes 2	(b) Yes 3	(c) Yes 1	(d) Yes 3
No 1	No 1	No 2	No 1
Sometimes 3	Sometimes 2	Sometimes 3	Sometimes 2

Task-orientated/motivator?

(a) Yes 3	(b) Yes 1	(c) Yes 3	(d) Yes 1
No 1	No 3	No 1	No 3
Sometimes 2	Sometimes 2	Sometimes 2	Sometimes 2

Risk-taker/indecisive?

(a) Yes 1	(b) Yes 1	(c) Yes 1	(d) Yes 1
No 3	No 3	No 3	No 3
Sometimes 2	Sometimes 2	Sometimes 2	Sometimes 2

Ambition/self-esteem?

(a) Yes 3	(b) Yes 3	(c) Yes 3	(d) Yes 2
No 1	No 1	No 1	No 1
Sometimes 2	Sometimes 2	Sometimes 2	Sometimes 3

Making an overall assessment

Examine your marks in each of the seven headings. The maximum possible score in each section is 12, the minimum 4.

10–12   An ideal, well balanced individual in the workplace. You are strong on qualities that will get you noticed as you are a natural leader.

7–9   You demonstrate high potential, but need to develop your self-confidence and become more self-assured.

4–6   A cautious individual who needs ongoing support and encouragement. You can improve your performance in this area and be successful if you have the motivation.

MAKING A PERSONAL ACTION PLAN

1. Complete a skills audit and assess your particular strengths.

2. Compile a personal charter which reflects your values and standards.

3. Analyse the power structure at work and devise a strategy which broadens your power base.

4. Complete the self-appraisal questionnaire and devise a strategy to improve areas of your performance where you scored lower than 10.

5. Construct a personal training plan prioritising your training needs.

6. Identify one publication that you intend to read in the next three months.

2

Working Effectively with Your Colleagues

UNDERSTANDING YOUR COLLEAGUES

The previous chapter examined some of the factors that can influence your level of motivation. Most theories about motivation point to the same truism, that everyone is motivated by a desire to meet their own needs. You need to look at your colleagues and try to identify the source of their motivation, distinguish the main personality types, and recognise some of the games they play in order to get noticed and meet their **higher needs**.

Identifying types of colleagues

While everyone you work with is unique and different, four main categories can be found. You should be able to identify those colleagues who have:

- social needs
- self-esteem needs
- self-actualisation needs
- power needs.

Colleagues with social needs
After satisfying their basic needs for paid work with a degree of job security, some colleagues with limited ambition see the workplace as an opportunity to satisfy their social needs. Their primary interest is to use it as an opportunity to make friends, share common interests, pursue a social life and even find romance.

Colleagues with self-esteem needs
Some colleagues use the workplace as an opportunity to solicit the attention they crave, whilst others seek recognition and acknowledgement of their talents. Their primary aim is to gain

recognition of their expertise or industrious activity from either their boss or colleagues, in the form of praise and recognition. This makes them feel good about themselves and boosts their self-esteem.

Colleagues with self-actualisation needs
Colleagues who have a powerful drive to achieve are said to be meeting their self-actualisation needs. They are often insensitive to how other colleagues and team members feel, and not unduly concerned whether their colleagues like them, although they expect to be respected. These colleagues find team-working stimulating and enjoy the challenge of achieving a difficult goal. They respond positively to pressure and deadlines, as this gets their adrenaline pumping, and they gain immense satisfaction from being part of a successful enterprise.

Employers generally value those with self-actualisation needs because they are committed to the organisation and align their higher needs with the company's objectives.

Colleagues with power needs
Some colleagues who need to feel important satisfy their power needs by exercising control over others at work. Being in control and having influence is all-important. For them power becomes addictive as well as seductive, because it also imparts a feeling of well-being. Controlling resources, including other staff, can become intoxicating and lead to some becoming workaholics. Others enjoy exercising power, manipulating others, being involved in brokering deals and the intrigue and politics of the business world.

Other considerations concerning colleagues

Many colleagues do not slot neatly into any one of these four categories, as their needs overflow into more than one. Human beings can defy attempts to pigeon-hole them.

One can speculate endlessly about colleagues who have need deficits in their private lives as to whether they are compensating for them in the workplace. For example, is an over-assertive colleague dominated at home? Is a workaholic escaping from an unsatisfactory home life? The answer can never be definitive.

BUILDING TRUST AND EARNING RESPECT

It is vital that everyone in the company works in harmony and pulls in the same direction. Working with most people involves a certain amount of give and take if friction is to be avoided. Everyone needs to exercise tolerance of colleagues' idiosyncrasies, mannerisms and eccentricities if unity is to be maintained.

Developing trust

Good relationships don't just happen; they take time to develop. Working relationships have to be nurtured and based on mutual trust.

The ingredients for success are in these ten golden rules:

1. Accept others in good faith.
2. Do not be judgemental.
3. Treat others as you like to be treated.
4. Take an interest in them as a person.
5. Respect the contribution they make.
6. Acknowledge their talents and achievements.
7. Be supportive and helpful.
8. Establish a good rapport.
9. Be loyal and generous towards others.
10. Always be positive.

Obstacles to building trust

Negative thinking and destructive attitudes are the curse of any business, and the source of most of the friction that occurs between colleagues.

Any of the behaviour included in The Pyramid of Obstacles (Figure 2) has a detrimental effect as it undermines trust, respect and good teamwork.

COMMUNICATING OPENLY WITH COLLEAGUES

Communication is as much about getting your message across clearly and accurately as about developing listening skills. It is a two-way process which involves learning to listen attentively and responding appropriately to what is heard. Care needs to be exercised that what you are communicating is fully understood by the other person, otherwise confusion results as the

Fig. 2. The pyramid of obstacles.

wrong conclusions are drawn and the whole exercise becomes counter-productive.

Most discussions between those in a managerial relationship tend to be formal, whereas the majority of exchanges between colleagues tend to be informal. Conversations between colleagues tend to focus on the following matters:

- information sharing
- sharing ideas
- giving advice
- making suggestions
- resolving mutual problems
- tackling training needs

- sharing the latest gossip about individuals and the organisation.

Much of the openness and rapport that develops in a company is due to the quality of relationships and trust that develops between colleagues.

Avoiding potential problematic areas
Barriers to effective communication arise when:

- messages get distorted in the formal communication chain;

- uncertainty develops about what the company expects from the team;

- communication becomes one-sided;

- a communication overload develops;

- trust breaks down between colleagues;

- a power struggle develops between competitive colleagues who seek to score points at each others' expense.

Most problems arise when members in the team lose sight of the overall objective and start to work in isolation, each pursing their own agenda. Once the team approach becomes fragmented communication suffers with disastrous consequences.

CREATING A SOUND BUSINESS TOGETHER
A sound business has to be receptive to change. It needs committed staff who are flexible, resilient and able to adapt to changing demands from management. The management team must exercise strong leadership and demonstrate their commitment to a policy of continuous improvement in a rapidly changing world.

Creating a climate conducive to innovation and development is challenging. The culture should be receptive to new ideas, which must be allowed to germinate and flourish. It is essential the team feels valued and involved if a sound busines is to be built.

Taking risks is part of the price of progress and remaining competitive in the marketplace. Risks can be minimised but not entirely eliminated. Managing risks should not be achieved at the expense of allowing relaxed, informal relationships between colleagues to thrive as this is at the heart of an effective business.

A successful business will include these elements:

- a flexible approach that encourages and rewards creativity
- an acceptance that risks have to be managed
- well-developed relationships within the team
- a commitment to investment
- a clear strategic plan.

Maintaining the correct balance

Most businesses face a dilemma between the need to maximise production and the need to invest in the future success of the business, because productive work generates income and is the life blood of the business. Failure to invest in research or to spot future trends can be fatal. Resources need to be allocated to ensure a range of new and improved products are continually coming on stream.

An efficient business will establish clear roles for each team member. This should identify colleagues involved in the following key activities:

- research and development
- creative thinking
- developing quality control systems
- informing people about what is happening
- providing feedback about individual and team performance.

Identifying sources of potential conflict

There is invariably a healthy tension between those involved in production and those engaged in research activities. Colleagues involved in manufacturing need specific competencies and a high detree of self-discipline including organisational skills. Innovators and ideas people, with high energy levels, often exhibit a dis-organised and chaotic approach.

The potential for conflict between innovators and producers is self-evident, therefore a high degree of mutual respect and tolerance is necessary.

A clear commitment to the overall goals of the business, coupled with an appreciation of the roles of individuals within the team, is vital; otherwise jealousies, tensions and misunderstandings occur.

WORKING WITH TECHNICAL EXPERTS

A multi-disciplinary team works most effectively to achieve a given objective when the outputs of the whole team are valued more highly than an individual's comtribution.

There are several issues to consider when working with any specialist or expert. Integrating them into an established team requires:

- recognition of their skills and knowledge
- acknowledgement by the team that they have a valid contribution to make
- full acceptance of them as a colleague.

Nurturing teamwork

Each member of a multi-disciplinary team needs to be in tune with the overall objectives of the business. These can only be achieved if good working relationships are nurtured through teamwork.

Managers need to foster ownership by the whole group. This means involving them in the consultation process, and ensuring they are kept informed of developments that affect them.

The following factors contribute to harmonious team-working:

- addressing identified training needs
- providing ongoing support and advice
- encouraging the use of initiative
- dealing with obstacles to effective team-working.

Colleagues with a particular expertise can become dysfunctional and ineffective if they are constrained by bureaucracy, encounter inflexible working practices, or experience antagonism from their colleagues.

The key to working successfully with experts is to accept them on an equal footing and integrate them fully into the team.

RESOLVING CONFLICT

There are many sources of potential conflict in the workplace. Every manager must deal effectively with complaints and grievances. This includes responding appropriately on an emotional level, to the frustrations experienced by colleagues.

An understanding of the main areas for potential discontent and unrest within a group is valuable. Figure 3 identifies the main sources of conflict, together with the debilitating effect they can have on colleagues. These areas of potential conflict do not include the added problem of contrasting personality types.

We all periodically encounter colleagues who are:

- abrasive

- intolerant

- rude

- sarcastic

- antagonistic

- provocative

- tactless.

This list is by no means exhaustive and you would be forgiven for wondering how anything ever gets done at work!

Identifying work rage

The cumulative effect of one or more sources of conflict, coupled with the inevitable rubbing points that occur due to the human element, can lead to the equivalent of 'work rage' (see Figure 3). This is when colleagues have reached boiling point and are unable to contain their emotions or exercise self-control. It is an intense form of stress, which in its most extreme form results in criminal action and certain dismissal.

The initial symptoms are not difficult to recognise:

- a colleague who is seething
- extremely negative behaviour
- a naked display of hostility
- covert sabotage.

In extreme cases the result is:

- destructive behaviour against property in the workplace
- an assault on the offending person
- an act of deliberate sabotage or arson.

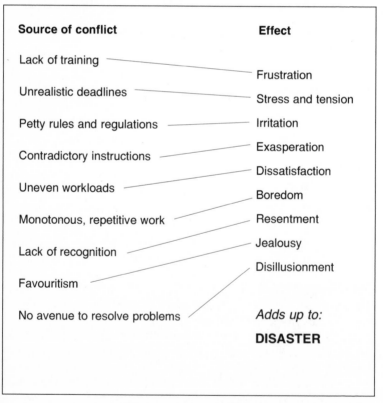

Fig. 3. Sources of conflict.

Defusing conflict

There are several stages in the process of forming a cohesive group. The initial stage is when colleagues are getting to know each other. Roles becomes clearly understood within the group, the working culture is appreciated and everyone is clear about the goals of the business.

Each group member will develop different expectations about each of their colleagues, and view some in a critical light. As the group becomes established these irritations and conflicting expectations magnify and surface, which can lead to conflict. If the group members acknowledge these difficulties and collectively seek to reduce rubbing points, they will emerge from this stage having developed greater trust, openness and cohesiveness. Mutual adjustments will be made to the group dynamics and the culture will change accordingly.

Working with Theory X and Y

Another source of potential conflict is identifiable in Douglas McGregor's theory of motivation, known as **Theory X** and **Theory Y**. This research suggests there are two distinct groups of people at work.

- Theory X people dislike work, see it as a necessary evil and consequently try to avoid it if at all possible. Such people need to be closely supervised and directed.

- Theory Y people are well motivated and have a tendency to welcome increased responsibility. Such people need minimal levels of supervision and guidance.

Colleagues with opposing attitudes like these are never going to work well together because the Theory X people will resent the minimalist approach of their Theory Y colleagues. Unless the Theory Y group is able to exert a positive influence on the working culture, tension will always exist.

McGregor's theory of motivation is an over-simplification of what happens in the real world of work. Undoubtedly there are some Theory X people whose behaviour cannot be modified or changed. However, by exercising good leadership, encouraging good communication and positive interpersonal skills, the culture can be modified and positive change introduced in an incremental way, and a winning team developed.

BEING PART OF A WINNING TEAM

Everyone wants to be part of a winning team where enthusiasm, motivation, and self-belief is high and team members are keen to support and co-operate with each other. Colleagues in winning teams are easily identifiable as they channel all their efforts into maximising output and achieving high standards.

These ten characteristics can be found in a successful team:

1. Open communication between members of the team.
2. Receptivity to new ideas.
3. Mutual support.
4. Cohesion and harmony.
5. Concern for the welfare of other team members.
6. Strong commitment to achieving high standards.
7. Knowledge, adaptability and multiskills.
8. Loyalty and commitment to realising the goals of the business.
9. Honesty with each other.
10. Recognition of the contribution of each team member.

You cannot be part of a winning team unless you have a team leader who is committed to helping the team work together, who develops the talents of each team member and represents the team in a credible way. The next chapter explores the importance of managing upwards and working for a winner.

CASE STUDIES

Joy, store manager

Joy is in her early 20s and has worked for the same company for five years. She is out-going, friendly and co-operative as well as very ambitious, extremely capable and conscientious. Her regional manager, who is acting as her mentor, believes she has the potential to rise to chief executive, providing she undertakes advanced management training. Joy is popular with all her colleagues and leads an active social life. She undertakes voluntary work in the community with disabled children, organises outings and goes on day trips with them in her time off. She is currently dating a manager who works in head office, but has no plans to get married and have a family.

Faye, artistic director

Faye is in her late 30s, married but with no children. She is an intelligent, highly efficient career woman who has built an enviable reputation as artistic director in the animation department of the BBC. Her career has allowed her to gain recognition of her artistic talents, and she wishes to broaden her experience and develop the skills of promising newcomers into the industry. A large part of her job satisfaction comes from using her artistic talents fully, and having her expertise acknowledged and valued by her professional colleagues.

Jonathan, sales representative

Jonathan is 28, single and works as part of a double-glazing sales team. He is highly committed to the business and works hard to achieve the best individual monthly sales figures. He enjoys the stimulus of working in a competitive environment and thrives on the challenge to exceed the previous year's sales target. Jonathan is well respected by his sales manager and consistently generates the largest number of orders. However, his single-minded approach has made him unpopular with some colleagues, who describe him as insensitive and with a ruthless streak.

MAKING A PERSONAL ACTION PLAN

1. Examine your motivation with a view to identifying your career aspirations.

2. Audit your skills by listing your strengths, weakneses, opportunities and threats.

3. Using your skills audit, prepare yourself a training plan.

4. Plot a career path, with time boundaries, based on a realistic appraisal of your potential.

5. Review your record of achievement in your present post and consider when is the most opportune time for a career move.

3

Managing Your Boss

ANALYSING YOUR BOSS

Your relationship with the boss is crucial. Work at managing the relationship, rather than trying to manage your boss. Aim to make the relationship mutually beneficial.

Most bosses are ordinary, reasonable people when you meet them socially. In the work situation their priorities and interests may be different from your own, for reasons that may not be immediately apparent.

Being an accountable boss
Your boss is responsible for the work of the whole team, and is accountable and answerable for your work, even your mistakes.

This responsibility can be onerous and can make some bosses more difficult to deal with than others. Coping effectively with your boss means developing a relationship which is based on mutual trust, respect and support. Do what is best for the organisation, as your future success is inextricably linked to its success.

Analysing your boss means focusing on three critical areas of your professional relationship:

- appreciate the aims and values of your boss

- recognise their strengths and weaknesses

- understand the pressures they are facing.

Assessing the aims and values of your boss
Take time to understand the aims and values of your boss, in order to discover their personal and professional goals. This will make you less inclined to criticise their performance.

Your attitude, which is always a revealing clue to what you are really thinking, should be positive and tolerant of any weaknesses you uncover. Adapt your style and approach so that you are compatible with your boss, without becoming a clone.

Asking the key questions
Some of the questions you need to answer are:

- Are they ambitious?

- Do they feel secure and have self-confidence?

- How do they judge success?

- Do you understand what the boss expects from you?

- What criteria does your boss use to assess performance?

- Can you respond appropriately to the demands made upon you?

- Does your boss appreciate open and frank discussion?

- Is your boss able to delegate?

- Does your boss have to always feel in control?

- Are they autocratic and dictatorial?

- Are your boss's values and standards ethical?

- Can you work harmoniously with your boss?

Knowing your boss's strengths and weaknesses
Ask yourself:

- Does your boss understand and appreciate complex questions?

- Are their interpersonal and communication skills well developed?

- How about are they to contribute practical solutions to operational problems?

- Is your boss able to take a strategic view of the business?

- Would you describe their approach as adversarial?

- Do they enjoy conflict?

- Would your boss avoid tackling difficult issues in case they upset someone?

- Are they popular and well liked by all the staff?

Learning to be supportive

Appreciate your boss's strengths and tolerate their weaknesses. Nurture this important relationship and ensure it is productive and mutually satisfying by:

- being open and honest in your discussions;

- establishing a good rapport;

- offering fair and balanced advice, particularly when commenting on the performance of colleagues.

IDENTIFYING PRESSURES FACING YOUR BOSS

Keep one step ahead of your colleagues by developing lateral thinking and a greater understanding about the business. This will enable you to contribute an added dimension in discussions. Most of your colleagues will tend to focus on strategies which further their best interests in the short term.

A bureaucratic organisation which rigidly follows laid down procedures stifles initiative, suppresses creativity, undermines morale and in time destroys an enterprise culture. If a blame culture is allowed to develop your boss will avoid taking risks and being exposed to criticism.

A highly competitive environment generates adrenaline and excitement, but also encourages ruthless behaviour. This can lead to a culture developing where a caring for colleagues ethos is undervalued or perceived as weakness.

The most stressful activities that face a boss are when they have to meet an extremely tight deadline or have to sack a colleague. Deaths from heart attacks or heart disease are significantly increased when bosses face these particular pressures.

Checking your boss's stress levels

Monitor the stress levels of your boss. Their relationship with their line manager can be a source of pressure and additional stress. At an opportune moment subtly encourage them to reduce their stress levels. Recognise the signs and offer to take on some of the load. A well-timed offer of help may assist your career prospects enormously.

Well-proven measures to reduce stress include taking regular exercise, reducing excessive weight; and regular checks on blood pressure and cholesterol levels give early warning of potential problems.

The following questions are a checklist for monitoring the pressures facing your boss:

- Which of your boss's incentives and perks depend on them personally achieving certain targets?
- Are they subject to a profit-sharing scheme linked to the overall productivity of the team?
- Do the management team hold your boss in high esteem?
- Is your boss seen by peers as a valued colleague?
- Are you boss's motives distrusted by peers because they are considered self-serving and selfish?
- Can you help improve the credibility of your boss?

Helping to reduce stress
A successful and stress-free relationship with your boss will:

- be relaxed and professional
- blend differences in style
- complement each other's strengths and weaknesses
- result in a united approach.

A partnership approach involves sharing ideas through open and honest communication. This professional relationship should develop your skills, your knowledge base, further your career prospects and lead to successful business outcomes.

ASSESSING YOUR BOSS'S MANAGEMENT STYLE

Management style influences staff relationships and contributes to the development of a productive climate in the business. Styles of management can vary enormously. Your boss may be formal and bureaucratic with everything done according to laid-down procedures, or informal and relaxed with a flexible approach.

A consultative and participative style of management en-courages contributions to the decision-making process. It seeks to find a balance between achieving the goals of the business and maintaining staff morale, which creates the climate for colleagues to develop their potential.

An authoritative and dictatorial managerial style is evident in a business where the focus is solely task-centred. Your boss may be over-demanding, with high expectations, autocratic and exploitative, or patronising and paternalistic.

Assessing the ideal boss

Everyone's ideal boss is different. A boss who is reasonable and understanding is likely to be a good motivator. A good leader is both stimulating and visionary; someone who is supportive and encourages everyone to contribute their best performance.

Your boss may be directive and allow you little opportunity to influence events. Others can spend much time consulting everybody, making them feel involved, but fail to achieve anything tangible.

Evaluating management style

Your requirement is for a boss who is consistent and fair. Check how well you understand your boss's management style:

- Can you anticipate how they will deal with a problem?

- Are your contributions acknowledged and valued?

- Do they consult you about matters that affect you?

- When difficulties arise, are your actions supported when you act appropriately with delegated authority?

- Does your boss receive support and backing from line management?

Accurately predicting how your boss will react in a given situation is important. This reinforces your authority, boosts your self-confidence and enables you to feel in control when they are not around.

Do not adopt your boss's management style. Recognise and appreciate different styles of boss, but in the final analysis be your own person.

RECOGNISING DIFFERENT TYPES OF BOSS

A boss who believes the basis for a good relationship with their team is open communication will probably be a good motivator and skilled at sharing the vision.

Working for a good boss
Those who get the best performance from their team fall into one of the following three categories.

The pro-social boss
This is a leader who shows an active interest in developing the potential of colleagues they manage, and encourages them to work effectively as a team.

The boss with good cognitive skills
They have an extensive knowledge base, are innovative and have excellent persuasive skills.

The boss with high positive expectations
They set high standards for themselves and others, and have full confidence in the capabilities of the team. They motivate team members to take a pride in their performance and achieve their full potential.

Anyone working for one of these bosses has little cause for complaint. Everyone tries hard to impress a good boss, which makes it more difficult for you to stand out from the crowd.

Working for a difficult boss

Having a difficult boss can be a very exasperating experience. Many have numerous human failings, including irritating faults and skill deficiencies. Most bosses have at least one of these. Look for another job if you are working for someone who has most of them; life must be unbearable!

The poor listener
A rigid outlook, unreceptive to the contributions others make. With tunnel vision and an inability to appreciate the bigger picture, they often have preconceived ideas about the outcomes before embarking on what they see as the tedious business of consultation. Influencing them requires infinite patience coupled with a good sense of timing.

The adversarial boss
May insult you, or try to humiliate you in front of colleagues. They are basically insecure and looking for ways to boost their flagging self-confidence. They abuse power to gratify their needs and boost self-esteem. Stand up to an adversarial boss otherwise you can experience extreme stress and rapidly become demoralised. Learn how to be assertive as opposed to being argumentative. Make it clear you expect to be treated fairly. Have a discussion in private where you won't be interrupted, and help your boss understand how to get the best performance from you.

The unfeeling and uncaring boss
The self-centred boss shows little interest or concern for any staff. Their insensitivity and lack of social skills are self-evident, and account largely for the poor performance and low morale of the team. Colleagues need to be treated as individuals with feelings, needs, desires and career aspirations.

The task-orientated boss
This boss can be aggressive, forceful, argumentative, domineering, pushy and bombastic. Be assertive and, in extreme casees, document their bad behaviour and face them with your dossier, indicating a willingness to take matters further. Do nothing and you risk being ground down and your self-confidence suffering. They seem unable to understand why the quality of work is poor, staff feel aggrieved, fail to be co-operative, appear sullen, even aggressive. In extreme cases some colleagues will resort to sabotaging efforts to run an efficient business.

The angry and impulsive boss
This boss is impatient, easily loses their temper, readily gives vent to feelings and resorts to swearing without provocation. Like a spoilt child they are best ignored when sounding off. Normally they come down to earth quickly once they have let off steam and regained composure. Choose the right moment to make a measured response, particularly if any criticism made of you is unwarranted.

The controlling boss
Unable to trust anyone or delegate any authority. Coping with an insecure boss takes time and infinite patience. Some, damaged by earlier organisational experiences, never recover. Contain your

frustration. If you show your irritation, it will be interpreted that you have an attitude problem, and further evidence of the need for closer supervision.

The autocratic boss
An inhibiting effect on the team, stifles open communication, antagonises subordinates, provokes opposition and attracts hostility. Autocrats are often arrogant, self-indulgent people who display a superior attitude as a mask for their basic insecurity.

The ruthless, power-seeking boss
Hungry for power and recognition they take the credit for any good ideas, exploit team members and ingratiate themselves with superiors. Often a workaholic with a deep-seated inferiority complex, they are driven by the need to prove they are better than everybody else. They lack insight and are totally consumed with meeting their own needs. This boss inspires real fear, so be wary and do not give anyone ammunition they can use against you. A vulnerable colleague may try ingratiating themselves at your expense, in order to survive.

The blaming, critical boss
Fails to give any positive feedback. Whenever anything goes wrong they apportion blame. 'The boss is always right' is their maxim. Managerial authority would be seriously undermined were they to admit to having any human frailties. Your survival strategy is simply to keep out of the firing line and curtail your natural enthusiasm to use initiative. When exercising delegated authority, make sure you have a clear brief and avoid tackling high-risk problems. Any failure will certainly be entirely your fault! Do not expect to be appreciated even when your perform-ance is outstanding.

The over-promoted boss
Tends to be anxious, lacks self-confidence and is indecisive. Un-comfortable with managerial responsibilities, especially when the going gets tough, they refer any problems to head office for a decision. If recently promoted, there is a possibility that in time they may grow into the job. However, some still exhibit these traits after several years. Be patient and supportive, although your contribution may not be openly acknowledged in case it is seen as an admission that you are more qualified for the job than they are

(which may be true). In time they may trust and rely on you, which gives you considerable influence and power.

The cowardly boss

Avoids taking unpopular decisions and appeases assertive and hostile team members. Beware of their tendency to reverse a decision when faced with resistance, as they always take the line of least resistance. If their own neck is on the line they act out of character in a desperate bid for survival. Take care, when they reverse a decision, that you are not left out on a limb or with egg on your face and have to make a humiliating public u-turn. Try to distance yourself from the decision-making process whilst maintaining your professional and personal credibility.

The fanatical boss

The agenda involves introducing a religious dimension into every work conversation. They are insensitive and intolerant of other religious faiths, and unwilling to engage in rational argument, but believe they have a responsibility to be evangelical in the workplace. A boss with strong political convictions, or a football fanatic, is easier to handle. Disclose you have similar interests; let slip they are your favourite team, and you earn valuable Brownie points.

The bullying boss

Bullies come in a variety of guises and are often charming in public but vindictive in private. Bullies will humiliate you and use criticism to maintain control. They are constantly nit-picking, marginalise certain individuals, have favourites, and may shout and scream without warning. Resist the temptation to do anything unlawful to them or their property!

Successful strategies

Be adaptable and determine an action plan that enables you to cope effectively with the problems a difficult boss poses. Depending on your personality and disposition, pursue one of the following six strategies:

(1) Ignore your boss's behaviour.
(2) Accept and tolerate their behaviour, but adapt your response to one that complements their behavioural traits and continue to be supportive.

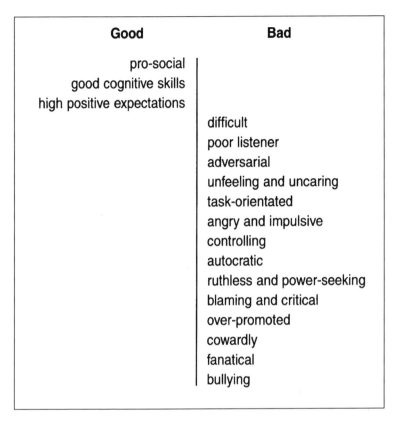

Good	**Bad**
pro-social	
good cognitive skills	
high positive expectations	
	difficult
	poor listener
	adversarial
	unfeeling and uncaring
	task-orientated
	angry and impulsive
	controlling
	autocratic
	ruthless and power-seeking
	blaming and critical
	over-promoted
	cowardly
	fanatical
	bullying

Fig. 4. Different types of boss.

(3) Refuse to accept difficult behaviour, be assertive and state clearly where the boundaries lie.

(4) Tolerate your boss's behaviour in the short term, until you have secured alternative employment and a positive reference.

(5) Attempt to influence your boss to modify their approach, using humour, your persuasive skills and peer group pressure.

(6) Complain to your boss's manager. They can exert pressure and oblige your boss to modify their behaviour. The possibility of having to appear at an industrial tribunal, defending the indefensible, can work wonders.

HANDLING MULTIPLE BOSSES CONFIDENTLY

In some organisations you have a normal line manager but are accountable to a specialist functional manager for technical or professional aspects of your work.

In a business the chief executive is responsible for the day-to-day running of the business but accounts to the board of directors on a regular formal basis. He or she also maintains a close working relationship with the chairman.

Having multiple bosses, in the form of several line managers or reporting to a committee, means it is essential to clarify responsibilities and agree priorities with all concerned. By co-ordinating action you can maintain control over your workload.

Competing priorities with multiple bosses

Problems often arise because your bosses have limited knowledge of each others' work and have competing priorities. The result is too many demands are made, in the mistaken belief you work for them alone. This three-point plan can help you determine priorities:

(1) Create opportunities for your bosses to meet and agree their priorities and work schedules.
(2) Help them to appreciate all the demands on your time and be realistic about what can be achieved.
(3) Do not play them off against each other or exploit the fact that none of them knows each others' priorities.

Your sole motive must be to control your workload and determine your own priorities, otherwise you may be seen as a manipulator and untrustworthy. Cultivate everyone whose co-operation and goodwill you need to achieve your objectives.

HELPING YOUR BOSS TO BUILD THE BUSINESS

Your boss needs to be convinced of your unswerving support.

Showing you are trustworthy

The following four-point plan will convince them you are trustworthy:

(1) demonstrate you are indispensable

(2) always be loyal
(3) be supportive
(4) do not antagonise colleagues.

Demonstrating you are indispensable
Talk regularly to your boss, appraise them of your skills and encourage them to let you prove your worth to the business.

Being loyal
Do not criticise and gossip about your boss to colleagues. Not only is it unprofessional, but it gives rivals ammunition to discredit you with your boss. This undermines all your previous good work and exposes you as a hypocrite to colleagues.

Being supportive by not being a 'yes man'
Many bosses value having someone they respect who they can use as a sounding board in the privacy of their office. Offer honest advice and your opinion, as this allows them to test out their ideas and benefit from your reaction.

Avoiding antagonising your colleagues
Support colleagues, and be open about your relationship with your boss. Otherwise they will mistrust and ostracise you, which is counter-productive.

Developing competitive strategies and managing change
The world of commerce and marketing does not stand still. The ability of a business to embrace change is crucial to its survival. A business needs a flexible organisation and an enlightened management in tune with the realities of the changing market place. It has to be able to motivate and enthuse its staff to face fresh challenges, like launching new products, if it is to survive.

Managers competing to survive, or fighting to maintain market share, can become aggressively competitive. Often it is assumed that a competitive spirit amongst the staff is good for the company, but this is rarely borne out in practice. A very competitive boss is likely to have high power needs and perceive situations as 'win-lose' rather than as opportunities to pursue collaborative strategies. This undermines group cohesion and can adversely affect productivity by raising stress levels.

Managing change

Managing change is stressful because the team is less confident and success is not assured. Paradoxically, the key to developing a competitive business strategy is to discourage the destructive competitive culture that can develop amongst colleagues. Strategies should be based on rational marketing criteria:

- analyse the market

- objectively appraise the product range

- conduct market research.

Formulating a strategy to implement change can include conducting a **SWOT analysis** of the company's potential. This means listing the **strengths and weaknesses**, evaluating the **opportunities**, then identifying the **threats** that face the business.

IDENTIFYING OPPORTUNITIES AND SKILL DEFICIENCIES

Consider which of your boss's skill deficiencies you wish to complement. Next assess your strengths and weaknesses, then persuade your boss to recognise and use your talents.

Identify those tasks your boss avoids because he or she lacks the necessary competencies. Attend relevant courses that enable you to complement your boss's skills and you will soon be indispensable.

Accept fresh challenges and broaden your experience, networking with those who can advance your career. Always carry out your responsibilities impressively, and demonstrate your ability to a wider audience whenever opportunities arise.

Looking at your boss's deficiencies

Your boss may have any of the following skill deficiencies:

- egotistical

- an ineffective manager

- weaknesses

- serious problems.

All these make them a potential liability and can undermine the profitability of the business.

The egotistical boss
Always right, even when demonstratively wrong. They have a need to control everything and everyone. Always dissatisfied with the quality of work, this leads to frequent clashes with team members. They are manipulative, avoid taking the blame and think everyone is after their job. Often a workaholic, their attitude towards anyone they perceive as a potential threat is intimidatory.

The ineffective manager
Needs to be everyone's friend, but interferes in routine work, avoids tackling difficult issues and can never be found in a crisis. Their decision-making is poor, because they are too easily in- fluenced by stronger personalities rather than by rational argument. Sometimes their problem is health-related, but more often it is laziness; they have grown tired, become disillusioned and been passed over for promotion.

The boss with weaknesses
Wastes everyone's time, refuses to listen to ideas and is indecisive. They are adept at avoiding responsibility for failing to meet production targets. They lack vision, and take a very narrow view of the business like focusing exclusively on the profit-loss account whilst being oblivious to deteriorating staff morale.

The boss with serious problems
An embarrassment to the business and a potential liability, as they expose the organisation to expensive problems, eg industrial tribunals. Their attitude to staff is deplorable, and can include sexual harassment and racially prejudicial behaviour. They lack credibility with superiors who view him or her with disdain but lack the political will to take appropriate action. Unable to cope with the stress of work, have a chaotic domestic life and takes refuge in stimulants. Dishonest when claiming expenses and misappropriates other company assets.

Becoming assertive and resilient
Every area of weakness you identify in your boss requires a difference approach. Some, like the egocentric boss, have to be

tolerated, which is a test of your patience and resilience. Others' problems have to be confronted using an assertive approach.

An ineffective boss can be helped to feel more secure, but this may prove to be a frustrating experience if they lack the basic competencies to do the job properly.

The strategy of complementing identified skill deficiencies works with the boss with weaknesses, providing you adopt an assertive approach and negotiate a mutually beneficial outcome. You'll need to be tactful, loyal, persistent and have a good sense of timing if you are to achieve a satisfactory outcome.

Serious deficiencies, which raise ethical and moral dilemmas, raise special problems and have to be handled skilfully.

Being assertive with your boss
Do not confuse being assertive with being aggressive. It simply means standing up for yourself and believing you should be valued and your feelings respected.

Adopt a rational, calm, confident approach and outline clearly your concerns. This should always be conducted in private, preferably by appointment, thus avoiding interruptions and the possibility that your motives may be misinterpreted.

Avoid aggressive body language and maintain eye contact. Adopt a relaxed posture, smile and concentrate on achieving positive outcomes. Providing you are polite, respectful but firm (and remember who is the boss), being assertive will earn you respect.

COPING WITH YOUR BOSS

An aggressive boss can make you feel defensive. You may even feel aggressive and look for ways to get your own back. If you are left feeling powerless you are in danger of becoming a victim.

Adopting a submissive approach may encourage others to take advantage of you. This lack of respect can result in your ideas and views being disregarded, leaving you feeling under-valued and unwilling to make a positive contribution. You may become over-loaded with work, because you are seen as a soft touch, and your own work will start to suffer. Your sense of grievance will intensify as your stress levels rise and your frustration may boil over, making you irritable and bad-tempered.

A manipulative boss can appear initially to be interested in you. Once you recognise their compliments are a plot to flatter and manipulate you into compliance, trust breaks down. If you are left feeling foolish and gullible, it is tempting to seek ways of retaliating.

Adopting a successful strategy

An assertive approach requires self-confidence, but is an effective antidote to a difficult boss. Relax your body posture, as this helps you appear more confident. Let others know your priorities, preferences and needs. They will respect those who are open and direct with them. Colleagues may want to form alliances with you in order to achieve mutually beneficial aims. Be seen as a force to be reckoned with and someone who has influence and gets things done.

Believing in yourself

A firm belief in yourself is the first step to building your self-confidence and improving your overall performance. Persevere and be determined to achieve your goals. A poor self-image affects your perception of the world around you. It can appear hostile and unsafe, with traps set for the unwary. This attitude makes it hard for you to be receptive to positive messages, causing you needless anxiety as you become preoccupied with what others think about you.

Improving your self-esteem

Your self-esteem will improve as soon as you start taking a positive and realistic view of yourself. Play to your strengths and stop listening to any negative messages; self-deprecation can easily become a self-fulfilling prophecy. Actively seek feedback about your performance from your boss. Listen to their criticisms with good grace, but always carefully evaluate any feedback objectively. Ask yourself:

- Is this constructive and justified criticism of my performance?

- How do others see me?

Be sensitive to what others are saying about you behind your back. Be aware that gossip may come to your boss's attention and there is always someone who feels they can advance their own case by undermining your credibility. Take care to guard your reputation and good name at all costs. However, most bosses are worldly-wise and politically astute and always have an interest in cultivating individuals who wield power and influence.

Meeting your own needs at work

Cope effectively with your boss, and meet your own needs at work, by following this advice:

(1) Identify issues you feel strongly about.
(2) Take time to respond when tempted to react instinctively.
(3) Adopt an understanding approach, rather than automatically assuming others are trying to be obstructive.
(4) Avoid over-reacting to situations. Keep cool, irrespective of your own feelings.
(5) Be crystal clear about your personal objectives at work.
(6) Identify those who have the potential to frustrate your plans.
(7) Confront difficult issues and problems systematically, but on your terms. Don't fight battles on more than one front at a time. Focus on just one issue and maintain control, thus increasing the likelihood of a positive outcome.

NEGOTIATING SUCCESSFUL OUTCOMES

Take stock and assess where your power base lies within the business. For instance, if you are the salesperson of the year you have a powerful card to play if negotiating future bonus payments. Sources of power in an organisation are:

- control over resources

- knowledge about the business

- status in the organisation

- a staff representative role

- specialised training and expertise

- leadership qualities

- physical presence

- managers owing you favours.

Controlling resources

When you exercise control over scarce resources that others need and require your approval, you have a position of power. Controlling budgets, equipment, staff and other facilities gives you considerable leverage and influence.

Knowledge is power

Knowledge about the business confers power. This may take the form of inside information about the future plans for the business, or experience about the business culture which enables you to take well informed decisions.

Having status

Your formal position and status in the organisation carries with it prestige which is reflected in your job title and salary. In its own right this has little impact, unless backed up by other forms of power, like control over resources or delegated authority to make decisions.

Representing staff

Occupying the role of staff representative, with a mandate from the workforce, puts you in a position to exert leverage on senior management. Influential union representatives are treated with respect because senior managers do not want to invite aggravation by antagonising the membership.

Having expertise

Anyone with specialist knowledge and expertise, like a solicitor or accountant, can be influential. A professional background or technical skill is readily recognised, along with individuals who develop particular expertise. Advice is sought, and sometimes followed without question, if you have a reputation based on a specialised knowledge base.

Being a leader

Strong personalities often have natural leadership qualities. Your enthusiasm and ability to influence others makes you a force to be reckoned with. Your views and opinions are likely to be respected if colleagues tend to be influenced by your charismatic leadership.

Having physical presence

A powerful physique, together with positive and self-confident body language, can inspire confidence. It may also intimidate others into deferring to your wishes. Colleagues concerned about your potential to be a threat may treat you warily.

Networking skilfully

Helping colleagues with problems, socialising and calculated networking can lead to situations where others owe you favours. Those obligated to you are usually loyal when you need reciprocal support.

Handling negotiations

Negotiating from a position of strength does not mean looking after your own interest at the expense of others. On the contrary, open responsible behaviour which serves the best interests of the business is encouraged. Every negotiation has to be handled with sensitivity, and you need to demonstrate a willingness to compromise. Don't antagonise colleagues by being self-serving, otherwise the temptation to form alliances to thwart your ambitions may prove irresistible. Concentrate on utilising your specialised knowledge, expertise, control over resources and knowledge about the business, which is always valued and in demand.

WINNING WAYS

Managing your boss successfully requires tact, skill and good interpersonal skills. It is an ongoing process that needs persistence, determination and self-control. Even good bosses can be irritating and frustrating at times. The key to success with your boss is to keep the channels of communication open.

Finding a successful formula

The formula for developing a working relationship, based on mutual trust and respect, with your boss can be recalled by **SCAM**:

- **S**eek advice.
- **C**ultivate them.
- **A**void being a know all.
- **M**ake yourself indispensable.

Seeking advice
Knowledge is power, so tap into their knowledge bank. Seeking advice also massages the ego of the vain manager.

Cultivating them
No one reaches a position of power and authority without having acquired a range of skills, knowing the right people or having business acumen. Be sure to recognise, acknowledge and cultivate their expertise.

Avoiding being a know all
Be aware of your boss's weaknesses and identify the issues they feel sensitive about. Be careful not to pose a threat. Neither try to be too clever or risk outshining your boss in company. Whilst most bosses don't always fully recognise talent they will always notice a subordinate with an overinflated ego.

Making yourself indispensable
Be enthusiastic, committed, loyal and a problem-solver. Many bosses have blind spots and gaps in their knowledge base about which they feel insecure. Know who their rivals or enemies are, and find out if there are any problematic superiors. Be on hand at crucial times to be supportive. If you manage to make them look talented in front of those posing a potential threat, your loyalty will be appreciated and remembered.

CASE STUDIES

Ali is ambitious but has obstructive colleagues
Ali is 36, married with three children and keen to develop a successful career. He qualified as a social worker at Keele University and was quickly promoted to team leader after he gained a Diploma in Management Studies. Ali enjoys a good reputation and is seen as a high-flier by senior management. However, his colleagues appear to be jealous of him and try to obstruct and discredit him whenever the opportunity arises.

Nick has a boss who keeps interfering
Nick is 48, separated and experiencing serious financial pressures as he has two families to support. He lives with his partner and her three children in Worthing, and commutes to Brighton where

he is the manager of a nation-wide store selling footwear. His boss, the district manager, is always visiting and constantly interferes, despite the fact that Nick is meeting all the sales targets.

Vicky's boss is a workaholic

Vicky is 30, single and lives with her boyfriend, a sales representative. She teaches at a grammar school and was recently promoted to head of department. Her headteacher is a workaholic and expects his senior staff to be totally dedicated to the school. He regularly holds meetings in the evenings and seminars at weekends, which causes difficulties for Vicky. Her partner travels extensively throughout the country during the week and she resents work intruding on the little time they have together at weekends.

MAKING A PERSONAL ACTION PLAN

1. Analyse your boss's strengths and weaknesses.

2. Identify which of your skills can be developed thereby increasing your value to the business.

3. List your sources of power within the business.

4. Design a strategy to increase your power and influence.

5. Identify those colleagues with the ability and opportunity to frustrate your plans.

6. Devise a contingency plan to deal with obstructive behaviour.

4

Team-Working to Maximise Profits

UNDERSTANDING THE CORPORATE CULTURE

Every organisation and business has a distinct culture. This is based on shared beliefs, values and assumptions which have evolved over time.

The culture can be influenced by external factors, like a change in legislation, the effect of new technology, market trends and what competitors are doing. Internal factors that can have a significant inpact on the prevailing business culture are a charismatic and visionary chief executive.

Having a sound foundation

The components for building a sound business are:

- the **mission statement**
- the **vision**
- the **goals**.

Developing a mission statement

The core values of a particular business are articulated in the published mission statement. This states the **values, aims, objectives** and **principles** that underpin the business.

The mission statement should make clear the purpose of the company and help to shape the corporate culture. It publicly declares where the business is heading and should invoke a sense of pride, loyalty and shared identity by all employees.

A company is likely to have a positive public image and be successful if the public associate the business with a mission. The Virgin group is associated with being a dynamic and enterprising business striving to be the best; Marks & Spencer has a reputation for selling high quality products backed by a no-nonsense exchange of goods policy.

Having a vision

The vision statement tries to imagine what it would be like to have already realised your plans for the business. A business vision has to be shared and believed if it is to be successfully translated into action.

These qualities are often found in those who are committed to achieving the vision, said to be a **CHIP** off the old block:

- **C**reative

- **H**ighly motivated

- **I**maginative and proactive

- **P**ositive and productive.

The vision for the business should complement the personal aspirations of everyone working for the company. This can only be achieved if they:

- are actively involved

- are convinced it is desirable

- see evidence that senior management are totally committed to making it become a reality.

Setting goals

The tactics used to achieve the vision are to set **goals, objectives** and **targets**. Goals are the method used to achieve the vision in the long term; intermediate targets are objectives and targets are short-term aims.

Measuring performance against the goals is a way to demonstrate individual success, the achievements of a department within the company and the overall profitability of the business.

These goals can be expressed in a number of ways:

- levels of sales achieved in a given period

- increased profitability

- improvements to productivity

- an increase in market share

- the rate the business is expanding

- an improvement in the market position.

Setting goals should involve colleagues at all levels of the organisation, especially those who are responsible and held accountable for achieving them.

Having a value system

Values express the standard of behaviour that is expected from everyone working for the company. However, simply stating the values of the business will have no impact on the prevailing culture unless they are put into practice by every employee.

The value system should address issues like:

- integrity

- personal commitment

- customer care

- innovation

- commitment to continuous improvement

- standards of excellence

- equality of opportunity.

Aspirations and reality

The multi-national oil company Texaco has a statement of values which are to:

- treat each employee with dignity;

- provide opportunities for development and advancement;

- maintain an environment where employees feel free to provide an input into business decisions;

- improve the system;

- make a difference.

Unfortunately for Texaco a costly court case in 1996 involving a black employee highlighted the problems that face a company when it fails to live up to its own high standards of conduct.

This legal case established that Texaco's custom and practice discriminated against black employees and minority groups when promotion opportunities arose. The consequences were far-reaching, damaging Texaco's reputation and wiping $1 billion off the value of its shares.

Influencing the culture

There are several factors that can have a significant influence on the business culture.

The unwritten norms

This describes accepted, standard practice. It includes the quality of colleagues' relationships and how they actually treat each other. It covers workplace practices and whether it is customary for there to be areas of demarcation or long-standing Spanish Customs (custom and practice agreements).

Management style

The way managers lead their teams and use their authority to achieve results is called **management style**. Leadership styles vary considerably. Managers can be autocratic, task orientated, partici-pative or democratic.

Status conscious

This reflects the importance of rank in the organisation and whether certain perks, like company cars and mobile phones, are allocated according to the status of the individual within the company.

Paternalistic approach

A paternalistic culture emphasises the importance of reciprocated loyalty. This is often demonstrated by a comprehensive benefits package, job security, a non-contributory pension scheme and a career path where promotion opportunities are restricted to existing employees.

Degree of formality

This refers to office relationships which are conducted in a formal, detached, professional manner with the use of first names frowned upon. There may be a widely respected dress code, or the company may provide a uniform. Group 4 provides a uniform which is worn by everyone irrespective of rank, whereas in the retail trade a company like British Home Stores provides company dress to their sales assistants.

BRINGING THE VISION ALIVE

The vision should be vibrant, dynamic and alive. It needs to be communicated with conviction by a managing director who has an appreciation of the big picture and who knows where the business is heading.

The vision for a business must embrace the philosophy of the company, its principles, beliefs and value system. It should inspire everyone, give colleagues a strong sense of identity and make them feel valued.

A vision imposed from the top is counter-productive because it is likely to alienate colleagues rather than produce a sense of ownership. A shared vision can only develop if every opportunity is taken to consult colleagues. They should be actively encouraged to contribute, and their knowledge and experience used when reviewing the overall strategy. Involving colleagues means incorporating their ideas into the strategic thinking of the business.

Visionary leadership

The vision for the business should give all colleagues a sense of purpose. This follows naturally once everyone knows where the business is going and what they are supposed to be doing.

The key to achieving success in a forward-thinking company or organisation is strong leadership and a cohesive team. Colleagues who have been actively involved in the consultative process become:

* committed rather than disinterested:

* enthusiastic rather than cynical;

* in tune with the goals of the business rather than alienated and feeling undervalued.

Working together

A vision built on teamwork is highly effective and efficient. A teamwork approach can avoid energy-sapping power struggles developing.

The vision has to come alive and be translated into *action* through the ownership, enthusiasm and commitment of everyone, irrespective of their role, otherwise it remains lifeless.

A vision that is neither believable nor realistic is meaningless. It will be seen for what it is: empty, fine words. A vision that is ignored by everyone is irrelevant and counter-productive.

INVOLVING COLLEAGUES IN STRATEGIC PLANNING

A **strategy** is a plan that has been devised to achieve the goals of the business. Every successful business must develop a strategic plan.

The process of strategic planning is where the long-term plans for the future of the business are developed then written down. In order to plan effectively the business needs to have a clear vision about:

- the purpose of the business

- the goals or long-term aims it wants to achieve

- the ability to acquire the resources necessary to achieve these long-term goals.

Developing an effective strategy

Developing an effective strategy means identifying and exploring all the available options, then deciding which is the most important business goal to achieve.

Evaluating these options necessitates a careful examination of a range of issues, which includes:

- potential future markets

- developing new products

- the rate of return on investments

- prioritising

- resource allocation.

Strategic planning

The process of strategic planning calls for a systematic methodology where the various alternatives are calmly and rationally analysed.

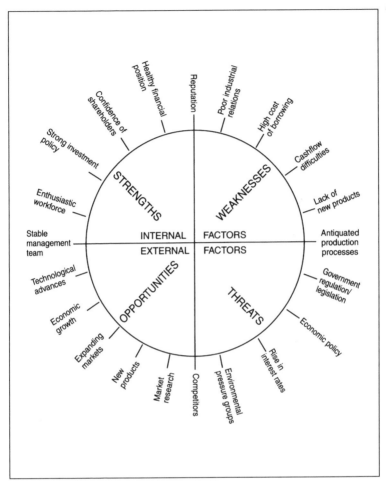

Fig. 5. SWOT analysis.

In many businesses strategic decisions are largely driven by significant external changes that occur in the marketplace. Changes to the government's planned legislative programme, a shift in economic policy, variations in interest rates, new products launched by a major competitor, future consumer trends or the level of confidence in the marketplace, can all mean making revisions to the strategic plan.

The strategic plan is crucial to every business. It means reviewing every aspect of the company to maximise productivity, improve market share, increase profits and secure the long-term future of the business. Strategic planning involves the following steps:

- defining the overall purpose;

- revising the objectives;

- undertaking market research;

- conducting a SWOT analysis (see Figure 5) which examines relevant internal factors:
  (a) the existing strengths
  (b) the weaknesses

  then evaluates the external factors facing the business:
  (c) the opportunities
  (d) the threats facing the business;

- reviews current policy and practice;

- revises and amends the objectives;

- produces a new three-year, rolling **business plan** high-lighting the important issues to focus on during the next 12 months;

- implements the new business plan;

- regularly monitors progress and achievements.

Involving others

Developing the overall strategic plan and the more focused business plan can improve decision-making, providing everyone is clear about where the business is heading in the longer term and the immediate future. Everyone who is a stakeholder and has invested resources in the business should be involved. This includes the following contributors as a minimum.

Investors
This covers **shareholders**, partners and senior managers.

Bankers
Any organisation which lends money and is interested in cashflow forecasts.

Operational managers
These are the key people who are responsible for making the plan work.

Employees
The enthusiasm and commitment of all your staff is essential.

Suppliers
It is important to retain their confidence and commitment, as well as adopting a flexible approach.

Regular customers
Your customers ultimately determine the success of your business. Remember the business maxim that 20% of the customers generate 80% of the profits.

The community
Sharing your plans with the media, taking them into the market-place and telling potential customers, can help to generate increased business.

WORKING WITH FINANCE TO INCREASE PROFITABILITY

In development a business plan attention must be paid to making accurate financial projections, as this is crucial to a successful business. The financial plan should cover:

- a marketing and sales strategy

- profit and loss forecasts

- cashflow

- capital expenditure plans

- identification of sources and types of finance

- stock purchasing policies

- management information systems.

Forecasting profit and loss
Most businesses lay great emphasis on forecasting cash flow, profit and loss. Managers need an accurate picture of how the

business is progressing so that potential problems can be identified and appropriate action taken.

The following example shows how to set out a simplified profit and loss forecast for the quarterly period 1 January to 31 March.

	Jan	*Feb*	*Mar*
Sales	850	850	700
Less direct costs			
Raw materials	165	165	125
Labour	180	175	110
Total direct costs	345	340	235
Gross profit	505	510	465
Less overheads			
Rend and rates	100	100	100
Heat and lighting	25	25	25
Telephone	120	110	85
Stationery	40	40	30
Administrative staff	100	100	80
Depreciation	65	65	65
Other	75	55	55
Total overheads	525	495	440
Net profit	−20	15	25

Understanding finance

A budget is the **plan** which is expressed in financial terms. It forecasts the income/revenue and expenditure/outgoings over the coming year.

A **balance sheet** acts as a snapshot of the assets and liabilities of the business.

The **profit and loss account** summarises the revenue and outgoings over a given period, and highlights any surplus and shortfall. It includes the **trading account** which shows the gross profits, and includes **overheads** which are fixed costs like wages, and **depreciation** of machinery and equipment.

Fixed costs are items like rental on premises, insurance premiums and wages. **Variable costs** are linked to the level of production, and include raw materials, energy costs and transport charges.

Financial management systems

A good financial management system is crucial to a sound business as it means:

- budget holders can be held accountable;

- delegation of authority within agreed limits can take place;

- up-to-date financial information is accessible to managers;

- effective monitoring and appropriate action can be taken.

Financial information needs

All budget holders need access to financial information which is:

- accurate

- clear

- well presented

- current data

- available on a regular basis.

Senior managers need to be able to take a global view of the business as a whole and receive an overall statement of **income and expenditure** figures for the previous month, the **year to date** figures and the **projected outturn** figures for the year.

A **budget profile** for he year should be compiled which anticipates seasonal variations. The budget shows the actual monthly income/expenditure and any variances against the projected figures. This means timely corrective action can be taken.

The financial information needs for departmental managers are less comprehensive. They require budgetary figures that relate to their cost centre. Too much financial data can be confusing and cause as many problems as a dearth of information.

Understanding the consequences of ineffective monitoring

Deficiencies in a financial information system make it difficult to monitor if progress is being made towards achieving **key performance indicators** (KPIs). The consequences of this are potentially very serious:

- the business plan cannot be effectively monitored;

- progress towards key objectives cannot be accurately gauged;

- appropriate corrective action is prevented;

- the board of directors cannot evaluate the profitability of the business;

- senior managers and departmental heads cannot be held to account;

- joint, co-ordinated action cannot be taken through the finance meeting.

BUILDING MORALE THROUGH BUDGETARY CONTROL

Although it is necessary to closely monitor and manage the budget effectively, each stakeholder uses different criteria to judge success. These conflicting expectations need to be appreciated if the morale of the company is not to be adversely affected:

- Investors and bankers expect a good return on their capital.

- Operational managers focus primarily on achieving sales targets and maximising production.

- Employees want job security, a regular income, with performance pay, bonuses or commission on sales in return for achieving performance targets.

- Suppliers seek a regular demand for their products and need their accounts settled on time.

- Regular customers demand a reliable, high-quality product which is readily available, delivered on time, competitively priced with ongoing after-sales service.

WORKING TOGETHER ON MARKETING TO MEET CUSTOMER NEED

Nowadays the whole process of launching a new product is carefully researched and a sizeable database collected before marketing decisions are made. Successful marketing depends on working as part of a team, with other managers, on a carefully thought out strategy which provides high quality goods to the selected customer group.

The core group in the marketing team should be the marketing manager, the research and development manager, the financial manager, the human resources manager and the production manager.

Out-smarting the competition

Although developing a brilliant strategy is invaluable, the way to outsmart the competition is by skilful implementation.

The key to making the business profitable is managing your team effectively. Building a cohesive team involves establishing trust, securing commitment, then turning that goodwill into a better performance. Achieving that takes time, effort, persistence and patience.

Putting people first and focusing on achieving customer satisfaction gives the business an edge on its competitors.

CASE STUDY

The expanding business

The North-East Engineering Company is a successful business which manufactures metal boxes. It wishes to expand its operation as the order books are full.

The Managing Director and his senior management group decide to have an away-day to review the vision, devise a new strategic plan and produce the business plan. The process of review involves all the major stakeholders including the employees. Following extensive consultation it becomes clear that diversifying into a wider range of products will secure the long-term future of the business and allow the company to expand activities in emerging export markets.

A new business plan is produced which includes a comprehensive financial plan, a detailed capital expenditure plan and the overall investment strategy. This is put to the Board of Directors by the Managing Director and shareholders after presenting the plan and explaining the commercial benefits of the revised strategy to them. A sophisticated financial management system is introduced which allows a wide range of accounting systems to be computerised, thus reducing costs and enabling improved monitoring to take place.

The implementation phase begins. New machinery and equipment is purchased and the workforce increases. Everyone receives appropriate training and care is taken to secure ownership of the vision and new goals from everyone in the company. As a result job security is assured, staff morale is high, and the workforce is positive and self-confident. The effect of this high motivation is increased productivity and a successful, expanding business.

MAKING A PERSONAL ACTION PLAN

1. Devise a personal vision which reflects your aspirations within the business.

2. Identify ways you can become actively involved in the strategic planning process.

3. Consider what skills you need to acquire in order to thoroughly understand the budgetary process.

4. Conduct a skills audit of your knowledge in information technology.

5. Devise a strategy in the form of a training plan which addresses any skills deficiencies.

6. Identify specific training courses which would help your professional development and explore whether practical support is available.

5

Being Accountable

ANALYSING ORGANISATIONAL BEHAVIOUR

Politics in the business setting is an inescapable fact. Managers serious about achieving their business objectives need to be aware of what is going on and avoid being manipulated by more astute and politically aware colleagues.

In business, colleagues form political alliances to ensure success in attracting resources and gaining co-operation from other divisions of the company. However, much political activity is self-serving, as some colleagues use politics to satisfy their need to dominate others, build an empire, create a favourable image and neutralise opponents.

Politics is about gaining power and influence. Most political activity arises from a need to resolve conflicts of interest, and overcome difficulties which are stumbling blocks to realising legitimate business objectives. Key questions you should address are:

- How can you use your influence to benefit the company?

- Are your personal ambitions consistent with the best interests of the company?

Identifying types of behaviour
The following types of behaviour can be observed in most companies and organisations.

Subversives
The desire to be anti-authority is directed by disaffected and disillusioned members of the workforce towards frustrating policy originating from senior management.

Bureaucrats
This is management's response to neutralise subversive subordinates. Managers introduce more rules, procedures and checks, to counter sabotage and make sure their will prevails.

Strategists
Their agenda is to change the structure of the organisation.
They know who takes the key decisions, who influence them
and cultivate the managers with real power in the decision-
making process.

Competitive rivals
Competitors are colleagues in other divisions within the company
who have control over resources. Their aim is to obtain a larger
share of the limited resources available to achieve their business
goals.

Empire builders
Colleagues intent on building a power base use the following
strategies:

(a) cultivating senior managers
(b) forming collaborative alliances with colleagues
(c) developing a particular expertise
(d) controlling access to information
(e) using their formal authority to exert influence
(f) manoeuvring to increase their control of human and financial
   resources.

ACHIEVING VERTICAL AND LATERAL INTEGRATION

Collaborating formally with colleagues in other divisions within
the company may require you to follow the established protocol.
In a bureaucracy this may involve channelling a request through
the appropriate line management chain.

A proactive company achieves co-operation across established
organisational boundaries by encouraging open communication
at all levels throughout the company. It recognises that some
business objectives will only be realised if colleagues adopt a more
imaginative and flexible approach.

Leading a project that involves colleagues from another
division means proceeding sensitively, negotiating introduc-
tions and gaining the necessary authority through line management.

Seeking vertical integration

Working as part of a team within the same division is more straightforward, but does involve understanding the basic dynamics of group working.

The team leader may be your line manager. They are responsible for creating a team identity, keeping the team focused on the terms of reference and completing the work within the time-scale.

Members of the team tend to adopt one of the following traditional roles:

The ideas person
A creative colleague with plenty of ideas contributes positively and stimulates other members of the group.

The team builder
They enjoy working with others and are interested in other colleagues' contributions. They tend to be popular and supportive, with an infectious enthusiasm which encourages others to contribute positively and wholeheartedly.

The devil's advocate
They are perceptive and have good analytical skills. Their value lies in being able to keep matters in perspective, their feet firmly on the ground, anticipate the counter-arguments and spot the flaws in your case.

The shaper
A shaper has plenty of drive and commitment and is not easily deflected from the task in hand. They do not recognise 'problems', only 'challenges' to overcome.

The finisher
They are persistent and determined individuals who see matters through to a satisfactory conclusion. Although they can be impatient with slower colleagues, they keep everyone focused on completing the task and meeting the deadline.

Avoiding a skills deficit

Every team needs colleagues with particular skills and qualities, if success is to be guaranteed. These competencies include:

- professional and technical expertise
- administrative ability
- operational and procedural knowledge
- policy awareness
- politically astute individuals
- lateral thinkers
- business acumen.

Seeking lateral integration
Collaboration across traditional departmental boundaries demands a multi-disciplinary approach. The role of the project leader is crucial. They must command respect throughout the company, otherwise some managers may become insecure, feel threatened, or become jealous and try to undermine the work of the team.

The project leader must be a good communicator, able to obtain the full co-operation of every team member and their respective line managers. They need to be politically astute, someone who commands respect throughout the company for their negotiating ability, interpersonal skills and positive style of leadership.

Achieving collaboration
Encouraging colleagues to collaborate can be achieved by convening meetings or forming working groups. Often existing informal relationships can be used to achieve mutually satisfying outcomes.

The necessary ingredients to achieve successful collaboration are:

- trust
- mutual respect
- compatible objectives
- reciprocal interests
- motivation.

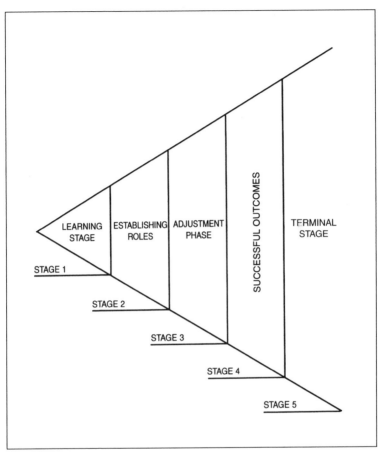

Fig. 6. The evolution of a team.

BUILDING AN ACCOUNTABLE TEAM

A successful team has a sense of mission, shares the same values, is mutually supportive and has team ownership of the business goals.

A stable team generates synergy more readily than a team where the membership is constantly changing. Synergy occurs when a positive rapport is established, and the energy and enthusiasm of the team is productively channelled.

Each team member hopes that working as a member of the group will satisfy their individual needs. The way team members relate to each other is known as **group dynamics**. They are constantly changing, depending on which stage the group has reached in its evolution.

The evolution of a team

A team evolves from the **LEAST** critical phase, where team members get to know each other, and graduates to the *most* productive phase where maximum productivity is achieved. The five distinct stages in the evolution of a team (see Figure 6) can be recalled as **LEAST**:

1. Learning phase. In the initial stage the team get to know each other, work out their role within the team and learn to appreciate their collective responsibility.

2. Establishing roles. Team members jockey for position, power and influence. This process leads to roles within the group becoming clearly established.

3. Adjusting. The team members make appropriate adjustments, work through their differing agendas and resolve how to collaborate effectively with each other.

4. Success. The most productive and successful stage, during which goals are realised. The team becomes enthusiastic, mutually supportive, working harmoniously to achieve the goals of the business. Individual emotional and collective achievement needs are fulfilled.

5. Terminal. The team disbands, or has to adjust to changes in its membership. Personnel changes affect the group dynamics and may result in regression to an earlier stage in the evolution of the group.

Achieving ownership

A cohesive team is productive and uses resources efficiently. A fragmented team which is competitive and fractious will be characterised by poor morale. A team that lacks ownership is distrustful, cynical and lethargic.

Once ownership is achieved, and a culture of collective responsibility is the norm, then you have a truly accountable team.

DEVELOPING A CULTURE OF COLLECTIVE RESPONSIBILITY

Most managers have a wide range of responsibilities and are over-loaded with work. This can be stressful, but learning the art of delegating avoids becoming burnt out. Creating more time to support members of your team is essential when developing a culture of collective responsibility. All managers need to learn a range of core skills which are:

- communicating clearly and succinctly
- lateral thinking
- the art of delegating
- exercising leadership
- a systematic approach to management.

Juggling skills

The art of balancing a range of different priorities is an essential skill for a manager to acquire. A good juggler keeps all of the balls in the air and concentrates on the most pressing problem.

A manager who has mastered this skill is able to pull rabbits out of a hat at the opportune moment and amaze their team and colleagues. Performing illusions and the occasional miracle, with reducing resources, are feats regularly demanded from managers. Managing unmanageable staff, achieving increased production targets with a paucity of resources and meeting impossible deadlines demand nimble footwork.

DELEGATING SKILLS

The first priority is to concentrate on the most important issue you have to deal with and ask yourself:

- Is anybody else capable of doing this piece of work?
- Would they require any training?
- Can they perform this task to the required standard?
- Are they available?
- Would they be willing to take on this additional responsibility?

Other issues to consider are:

- What level of skill and knowledge is needed to meet the prescribed quality standards?

- How time-consuming and costly is it to train colleagues?

- How much pleasure and job satisfaction do you get from performing this task?

- Will there be any adverse reaction from your boss if you delegate that task?

Conducting an honest self-appraisal

Delegating work does not mean you can abdicate responsibility. On the contrary, when you delegate work you must monitor, encourage and support the person carrying out that duty on your behalf.

1. The likelihood of making mistakes is greatest when assuming new responsibilities.

2. You are still responsible for the task you have delegated. It does not absolve you of the responsibility of ensuring it is completed on time and to agreed quality standards. This means making regular checks on progress and, if necessary, taking corrective action.

If there is no one readily available to delegate work to, you may have to cover either their normal duties while they receive training, or invest time in training them in their new responsibilities.

Acting as a mentor

Always seek to identify talent and nurture those who demonstrate potential. Delegating work to promising colleagues can demonstrate trust and a willingneess on your part to invest in them and help maximise their talents. Acting as a mentor to talented colleagues is an important part of succession planning. Hopefully, you will soon be moving on to bigger and better things.

Feeling indispensable

It is flattering to be considered an expert. This myth can be perpetuated by not sharing knowledge and skill, which denies others the opportunity to gain the necessary expertise. Ironically, by considering the needs of others you also help yourself. In time delegating work to others pays off, as it allows you more time to train colleagues and to be available to support them more effectively.

Delegating work enables you to concentrate on developing your own potential and career prospects by taking on more demanding and satisfying delegated duties from *your* line manager.

DELIVERING THE BUSINESS PLAN

An accountable manager has to be shrewd, develop a range of skills and a knowledge base which equips him or her to survive in the tough world of business.

To be successful you need to:

- Know about the formal power structure as described in the organisation chart.

- Appreciate the political realities of business life.

- Contribute effectively, by having a thorough understanding of group dynamics.

- Understand the LEAST process of how a team evolves.

- Develop a range of core skills which enable you to manage effectively.

Although these are the key skills you need as a manager to deliver your objectives in the business plan, success will only follow if you adapt to the prevailing company culture.

Regardless of the official equal opportunity policies and the standards of behaviour that are tolerated in the company, the managers who succeed in gaining promotion are those who conform to the company's business culture. Some bosses value this ability more highly than traditional managerial skills.

BUILDING A CREDIBLE IMAGE

Although there is some scope for individuality in a company, to build an acceptable image you must find out what type of behaviour is highly prized by the company. These are some areas to explore:

- Does your dress sense and general appearance compare favourably with other executives?

- Are your manners impeccable?

- Is your office or section smart, tidy and uncluttered?

- Do your personal habits, such as consumption of tobacco and alcohol, conform to acceptable company practice?

- Do you socialise with colleagues who will not detract from the image you are trying to project, bearing in mind you will be judged by the company you keep?

- Are the hours you work similar to other ambitious and successful managers?

- Is it usual with this company to take your full holiday entitlement, work late and attend at the weekends?

Finding suitable role models

Observe the working practices of successful managers whose behaviour conforms closely to the company culture. Every company has particular expectations of senior managers which they recognise and reward. This varies from one business to another, but can include recognising:

- creative people

- loyal, conscientious and hard-working employees

- sociable, easy going individuals with outstanding interpersonal skills

- those with a proven track record of achievement

- those who use their initiative and generate outstanding levels of revenue, orders or sales.

Improving your image

A proven way to improve your corporate image is to adopt a policy of continuous improvement. This demands considerable dedication and involves actively seeking feedback from your line manager. Ask for advice, and make sure you accept it graciously and try to act on it. If this involves adjusting your style of management, make changes in an incremental way and avoid making a dramatic u-turn. Otherwise this may back-fire and make your boss feel unsure about how you will respond in any given situation. They need a predictable, consistent performer who can represent them credibly, or conduct negotiations on their behalf with a client.

Questions to ask yourself

1. What image do senior managers have of me at present?
2. Am I clear about what profile conforms with the company's image?
3. Which of my special skills and qualities are not recognised?
4. Are there weaknesses I need to address as a priority?
5. Do I need to change or improve my attitude?
6. How can I adapt my behaviour, and do I need any help?
7. What can I do to project my full range of skills more effectively?
8. Would attending a training course correct any of these weaknesses?
9. Do I work hard to achieve business objectives and get results?
10. Am I honestly outstanding at my job?

CASE STUDY

Jonathan becomes an accountable manager

Jonathan works for a company which produces replacement windows and demonstrates he is an outstanding salesman by consistently generating the highest number of orders. He is well respected by senior managers for his enthusiasm and commitment to the company. He is not popular with his colleagues, who feel he is ruthless and insensitive, but Jonathan feels they are jealous of his high earnings. When his line manager leaves to work for a rival company, he is promoted and takes on the responsibility of Sales Manager.

Jonathan quickly realises he is accountable for the work of the whole team and that his continued success depends on being able to improve the volume of total sales and develop new markets. Initially he gives priority to enthusing and motivating his team, and helps one team member with personal difficulties which are distracting him from achieving high sales. Jonathan wins him over by relieving him of some of the work pressure and giving him extra time off.

He conducts a skills audit of the sales team and allocates resources from his budget to address skills deficiencies he has identified. Jonathan invests time in developing good lateral relationships with the Production Manager and his supervisors. This pays dividends when they devise a new system to streamline the ordering process, which results in the finished product being installed in the customer's home more quickly. As this also improves the cashflow of the company, and reduces bank charges, the Managing Director is delighted.

As the team becomes more cohesive and productivity increases, Jonathan finds he is able to spend time developing the managerial skills of team members displaying potential. He manages to delegate some responsibilities, which allows him to concentrate his energy on exploring new markets and expanding the customer base. Eventually be succeeds in securing a large contract with the local authority who decide to refurbish the entire council housing stock.

The company starts expanding, employs more staff on the production line and increases the size of the sales team. The team members, who are on a bonus scheme linked to the profitability of the company, are very satisfied.

Jonathan gains the respect of the Chairman of the Board of Directors, who is a major shareholder and sees him as a 'chip off the old block'. Over the next few years the Chairman becomes his mentor, guiding and helping him to develop the right corporate image. Under his guidance Jonathan develops his interpersonal skills to a high degree and extends business activity further into the public sector, where he wins several lucrative contracts against strong competition. Eventually he is offered a partnership in the company and is able to enjoy a comfortable retirement at 50.

MAKING A PERSONAL ACTION PLAN

1. Analyse who exercises power and influence where you work.

2. Write down the behavioural characteristics and core competencies the company requires from its managers.

3. Examine your corporate image critically and identify areas for improvement.

4. Identify a successful role model within the company.

5. Devise a convincing strategy that will secure you promotion within the next two years.

6

Working with the Board of Directors

WORKING WITHIN A BUSINESS STRUCTURE

Organisational charts are frequently used to describe the structure of a hierarchical organisation, clarify the lines of authority, and describe the professional relationships between different staff within a department, both vertically and horizontally.

These family trees (see Figure 7) show the formal channels of communication and the status of different employees. What they cannot show is the *informal* structure. This is the power and influence that individuals wield due to force of personality, networking skills and specialist knowledge.

Understanding the role of the chief executive

In a company the chief executive is the most senior executive with day-to-day responsibility for running the business. He is accountable to the chairman and the board of directors who formulate policy and provide guidance to the organisation's operational management.

The organisational chart in Figure 7 shows the management structure in a manufacturing company and its relationship with the board of directors. The chief executive leads a team of five senior managers who comprise the management team, who are supported by their middle managers and they in turn by the foremen, supervisors and others, all operating through a hierarchical structure.

INFLUENCING THE BOARD OF DIRECTORS

The board of directors is responsible for the overall success of the business. The directors devise the mission statement, create the vision, set the overall goals for the business and monitor performance through the chief executive.

The role of the board is to perform a leadership role and be accountable for everything that happens in the company. In

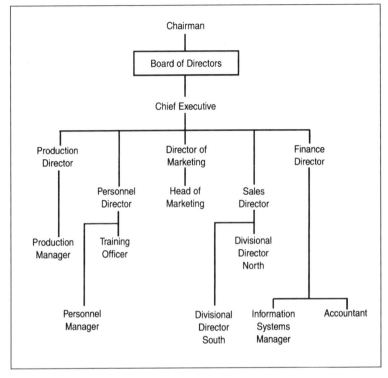

Fig. 7. The organisational chart.

theory the board of directors is very powerful, as it sets policy and delegates to staff the responsibility to carry it out. In practice, many boards meet infrequently and rely heavily on the staff for information and advice which makes them susceptible to undue influence. In the worst examples, the board ends up purely ratifying decisions taken by the chief executive and his or her colleagues.

Appreciating the role of the board of directors

The role of the board *vis-à-vis* the chief executive is a more complex relationship than the board deciding the overall strategy and the chief executive implementing it. The distinction is far more subtle and involves:

- a partnership approach
- the concept of added value

- anticipating and shaping future policy
- balancing the interests of different stakeholders.

The partnership approach

The cabinet model, where the Prime Minister is the first amongst equals, is a useful analogy when describing the relationship between the board and the chief executive and the senior management team. An effective partnership is forged when each concentrates on their respective functions and works to achieve common goals. This prevents duplication and confusion from developing and optimises the use of scarce resources.

Adding value to the business

The board must make a distinct and attributable contribution to the success of the business. Directors should not be obstructive, inhibit progress and innovation, or waste time by holding numerous time-consuming meetings. A board which does not add value to the business is a drain on the resources of the company.

Anticipating future policy

An effective board avoids crisis management by having foresight and a sense of direction. It should take a strategic view of events, interpret economic indicators accurately, identify investment opportunities and appreciate the significance of changes in the marketplace.

Balancing competing interests

All the stakeholders in a business have different expectations and make competing demands, which creates tension and can lead to conflict. A company with a weak board will find staffing issues dominate the company's agenda and will fail to strike a satisfactory balance between the needs of the different stakeholders.

Resolving tensions

The board with a clear mission statement and coherent strategy can help to diffuse these tensions. It performs a valuable function when it focuses on its principal responsibility of making sure the company is well managed and avoids becoming involved in the day-to-day management of the business.

IDENTIFYING THE IDEAL BOARD

The Cadbury Report recommended a model of good practice for a board with the following composition:

- Executive directors with specific responsibility for the marketing, finance and personnel functions.
- Three independent non-executive directors to safeguard the best interests of the company and its shareholders.
- A non-executive chairman who performs a leadership role to the board.
- A chief executive who reports to the chairman.

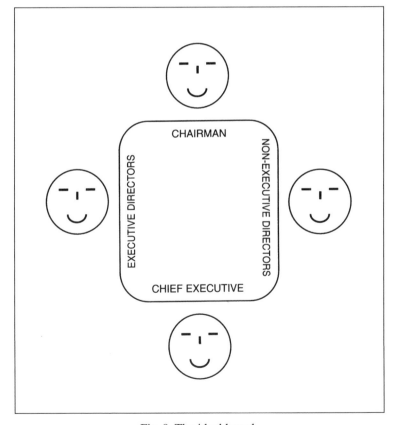

Fig. 8. The ideal board.

This model company (see Figure 8) also has a remuneration committee, made up of non-executive directors, who decide salary levels and allocate share options. All directors are elected by the shareholders (who own the company) and are responsible for running the business profitably.

BALANCING THE NEEDS OF SHAREHOLDERS

Shareholders – like employees, managers, suppliers, financiers and customers – are stakeholders and have an interest in the profitability of the company. The important distinction is that in the case of a limited company or a publicly owned company, the shareholders actually own the business.

Understanding the legal status

A limited company is the most common form of business, and is recognised in law. It has a legal obligation to be registered at Company's House and to file audited accounts each year. The owners, the shareholders, have a limited liability if the business fails as they only lose their original investment. A public limited company is similar to a limited company except that it can use the designation 'plc' after its name, and can float and trade shares on the Stock Exchange.

Shareholders' interests

The shareholders have an understandable interest in the profitability of the company and expect to receive a return on their investment in the form of regular dividends and a rising share price.

A company which fails to match its shareholders' expectations may find their loyalty is short-lived, and they simply sell their shares and buy others in a more profitable company.

Balancing different interests

Although shareholders have voting rights which they can exercise when major policy decisions have to be taken, the day-to-day running of the business is delegated to the board of directors. They recognise that the loyalty and interests of the shareholders can only be guaranteed if they ensure the share price continues to rise and the dividends are regularly paid. The market judges the profitability of a company according to its share price. The pay of some chief executives is linked to the share price, and they are part of a share option scheme and have a shareholding.

The needs of shareholders can be in conflict with an investment strategy which takes a long-term commercial view, because this may involve sacrificing short-term profits for a long-term gain. Balancing the needs of shareholders against those of other stakeholders means taking into account their need to maximise their return on their investment in the short term.

COMMUNICATING DIFFICULT DECISIONS

Good communication between managers and team members is essential if trust, good morale and productivity are to be maintained. Although there is no magic formula, communication skills can be developed if certain principles are followed. The most important thing to remember is:

- It is your responsibility to communicate effectively.

This means checking that the message has been received and understood.

Having a systematic approach

The essence of good communication is contained in the following four principles (see Figure 9), which can be easily remembered as they spell the word **FAST**:

- **F**ace-to-face
- **A**udience
- **S**imple
- **T**iming.

Face-to-face communications
This is the most effective way to communicate as it allows you to assess how well the message has been received and deal with any questions or concerns. Feedback is important, so respond to team members' feelings, respect their views and listen carefully to any criticisms or grievances they have.

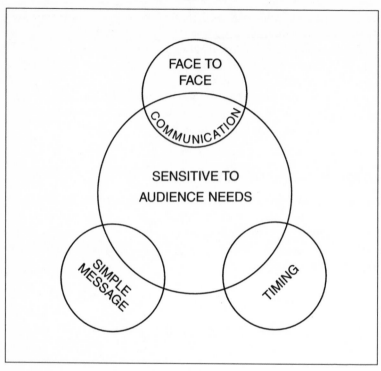

Fig. 9. Good communication is . . .

Audience needs
Be sensitive to your team's needs. People often reject, or go into denial, when they are presented with information they don't want to hear. Unpleasant news, like the likelihood of redundancies, may need to be repeated or rephrased before the message fully sinks in and the implications are appreciated.

Simple messages
All communications should be succinct and unambiguous. Use simple, plain language and avoid jargon or unnecessary technical language.

Timing
The timing of meetings is important. Colleagues will not listen attentively or make a constructive contribution if the meeting is scheduled to take place in their lunchtime, or when it is time to go home. A poor leader will deliberately hold a meeting at an

inappropriate time and attempt to suppress discussion if the subject matter is controversial. Consider your choice of venue and whether it is convenient to the majority of your team.

COMMUNICATING EFFECTIVELY

Unpopular decisions which adversely affect colleagues need to be handled carefully. Think about the best way to get your message across. Do not avoid meeting people because it is uncomfortable or embarrassing for you, but focus on how best to handle colleagues' feelings and likely reactions.

Difficult and unpopular decisions invariably provoke criticism and the search for a scapegoat. When facing this situation you have the choice of:

(a) holding a meeting
(b) seeing people individually
(c) using technology.

Holding a meeting
Every meeting should have a clear purpose and provide an opportunity for the team to be involved in the problem-solving process. A meeting may produce fresh ideas and original solutions, as well as provide team members with the opportunity to express their views.

Holding a meeting is more cost-effective than individual sessions, particularly if a large number of people have to be seen. A word of warning: many meetings are inconclusive, because they waste time by going off at tangents and fail to achieve the stated objectives.

Seeing people individually
A private meeting with a colleague allows a two-way dialogue and exchange of views to take place. It reduces the likelihood of misunderstandings and allows you to tailor the discussion to the needs of each person. The difficulty with seeing people individually is that it can be very time-consuming.

Using technology
The use of email can be valuable where speed is of the essence. It allows you to communicate with a large number of people in

different parts of the country, and gives them the opportunity to respond quickly. However, email is impersonal, and the recipient has to have access to the technology and be trained in its use.

Other formal methods of communication include sending a letter, memorandum or report. These methods are slower and the recipient is unable to make an immediate response.

Compiling a written minute of a meeting or a memorandum, or sending a letter of confirmation, is useful when you want to reinforce a verbal message.

Knowing your audience

Ask yourself who you are trying to communicate with. Knowing your audience is invaluable, and should help you decide on the most appropriate way to handle the situation.

A company faced with a disastrous fall in its profits may have little option but to make some staff redundant. It may use several methods to get its message across, depending on who it is communicating with.

Individual briefings
Stakeholders, like departmental heads and the bank manager need to be seen and briefed individually.

Convening meetings
A large workforce may have to be informed by convening a series of meetings and offering personal counselling later.

Formal communications
Customers and suppliers may be informed by a letter which explains the position facing the company.

Using email
The media, shareholders and the wider community may be advised by a press release, sent out by email.

In-house newsheets
Regular updates to the workforce may be by memorandum or through the company's newsletter, and aimed at combating rumour and speculation.

Making people redundant

Every colleague subject to a redundancy notice must be informed in private. The interview needs to be handled tactfully but in a business-like fashion. Social chit-chat should be avoided, and the time spent sharing the bad news and considering the implications in a professional way. You could conduct the interview as follows:

- Get to the point quickly.
- Be clear and honest but do not give false hope.
- Allow time for the facts to sink in.
- Rephrase the message, if necessary.
- Explain the reasons for the decision.
- Offer support and a further opportunity to discuss the matter.
- Tell them when the decision takes effect.
- Deal with the following practical issues:
  (a) their entitlement to redundancy pay
  (b) handing in or purchasing the company car or other perks
  (c) early retirement or pension arrangements
  (d) collecting their P45
  (e) outstanding wages and leave entitlement.

HANDLING CRITICISM OF YOUR BOSS AND COLLEAGUES

Taking tough decisions is usually unpopular. Having to make staff redundant or fire someone inevitably attracts criticism and results in bitterness. When the going gets tough be on your guard, as this is the time colleagues reveal their true colours.

Loyalty to the company is highly valued. Senior managers are expected to put the best interests of the company before their own personal needs. Companies equate loyalty with strong leadership and professional integrity. Setting a good example is crucial if good morale is to be maintained within the team.

Keep personal feelings and opinions to yourself because there are many keen to exploit cracks in the management team. Any disloyalty or indiscretions are ammunition for your enemies to use against you, including betraying you to the boss. Rivals may advance the fiction (at your expense) that they are loyal, selfless individuals, with only the best interests of the company uppermost in their mind.

Knowing the dangers of disunity

Disunity in the boardroom is fascinating for outsiders, and fuels endless speculation and gossip. However, it can be very damaging financially for a company, as shareholders take a jaundiced view of boardroom battles which distract senior executives from their principal responsibility to run a profitable company. Losing the confidence of shareholders and influential stakeholders can be disastrous. Once customers and suppliers begin to lose confidence it becomes very difficult to rebuild the company's reputation.

Tensions are inevitable in business, but these differences must be contained and managed otherwise the business suffers. At stressful times a common culture and sense of ownership is necessary to maintain a cohesive team.

Most disunity can be traced to leadership failures. Common causes of boardroom conflict are:

- Boardroom disagreements about the succession policy; for instance what happens when the chief executive or chairman retires.

- A fall in overall profitability prompting senior management to apportion blame.

- A company facing a take-over bid and creating tension, fear and high levels of stress.

- Major disagreements over company strategy, leaving some managers feeling bitter and nursing bruised egos.

Handling criticism

The tensions caused by professional differences can be handled effectively if the supervisor exercises leadership. A responsible leader should:

- concentrate on building a strong team;

- ensure nobody dominates the group;

- uphold the company's values and goals;

- avoid any criticism of colleagues or the board of directors;

- support existing company policy;
- relay legitimate team concerns to line management;
- seek advice from line management;
- be positive and supportive, but maintain the role of honest broker;
- be prepared to learn from the experience of others;
- seek to accurately identify the motives and hidden agendas of rivals who may be:
  (a) competing for advancement
  (b) disgruntled employees
  (c) passed over for promotion
  (d) negative and insecure
  (e) jealous colleagues.

Handling criticism correctly, blending humility with wisdom, may enable you to win over disaffected colleagues.

MAINTAINING CREDIBILITY

Managerial credibility depends upon the expectations of others being fulfilled. Your boss, colleagues, customers and the local community expect those who have responsible roles to conduct themselves in an exemplary manner.

Managers are the traditional arbiters of conduct and performance. They set quality standards, monitor production, review progress and are expected to personify the expressed values of the business. Any hypocritical behaviour erodes your moral authority and personal credibility. Once lost, the confidence of senior management rapidly evaporates.

Achieving high standards
Conforming to acceptable personal and professional standards builds credibility. Maintaining it depends on personal integrity and your ability to earn the trust of colleagues, which takes time. People judge you by your actions, not by fine words alone.

Losing credibility
Credibility and reputation can be seriously affected by failure. Failing to live up to your reputation, or not delivering your

promises, undermines the self-confidence and unity of the team and is a recipe for disaster. Any discrimination or unacceptable behaviour at work – like losing your temper, being rude to junior staff, sexual overtures to females, or being inebriated – is guaranteed to lose the respect of colleagues. It is difficult to regain lost credibility because people have long memories. No one likes looking foolish, appearing to lack sound judgement or seen to be backing a loser. A managing director who loses credibility and the confidence of the board of directors soon finds their position untenable and has to resign.

CASE STUDY

Joy's role as chief executive is short-lived

Joy is in her late 30s and has an excellent track record of business achievement. She is widely acknowledged to be an outstanding manager and is promoted to Chief Executive of The Triumph Engineering Company. She works very long hours and proves to be a charismatic leader. She is a good communicator, with well developed interpersonal skills, and persuades the Chairman and the Board of Directors to invest heavily and expand the business aggressively into new markets overseas.

The company experiences considerable growth over the next few years and everyone is committed to Joy's expansion strategy. The Board even considers raising the necessary investment by converting the company into a public limited company and floating the business on the stock market.

However, the recession hits the order book hard and the results over the last two years are very disappointing. Confidence in Joy starts to crumble, plans for further expansion are shelved and some staff have to be made redundant. This results in people beginning to openly question her credibility which undermines her authority.

The shareholders start grumbling about their poor dividends and become critical of the Board of Directors and clamour for the Chairman to resign. Relations between Joy and the Chairman become strained, neither accepting responsibility for the failed strategy and eventually the Board of Directors passes a motion of no confidence in Joy.

She realises her reputation cannot be rebuilt within The

Triumph Engineering Company and resigns her post, becoming a convenient scapegoat.

MAKING A PERSONAL ACTION PLAN

1. Consider how your style and techniques for communicating effectively with team members can be improved.

2. Analyse how developing your communication skills can be used to improve your visibility in the company.

3. Examine how cohesive the management team is, then identify sources of disunity.

4. Conduct a self-appraisal of your credibility, using a SWOT analysis, and identify any personal, professional and managerial shortcomings.

5. Devise a strategy to improve your credibility with:
   (a) colleagues
   (b) line management
   (c) the Board of Directors
   (d) other stakeholders.

7

Respecting Professional Boundaries

MANAGING WITHIN A BUSINESS CULTURE

The business world is highly competitive and the pressure to succeed is intense. Every stakeholder is looking for a return on their investment.

Anyone in business with career aspirations has to compete with other talented colleagues. Doing your job well is not sufficient to guarantee your next step up the ladder. Survival or success depends on the ability to understand, absorb and master the business culture. This culture can be defined as the accepted **norms** or **values** of the company, and which you disregard at your peril.

Some companies value punctuality and colleagues who work long hours. They may not be the best salesmen, but they conform to a work ethic that is highly valued by the company.

Meeting expectations

Some colleagues are dismissive of those whose 'face fits'. The truth is they have learnt to be flexible and adapt to their employer's wishes and expectations. The phrase 'he who pays the piper calls the tune' is as true today as ever. Employers expects those they recruit to be willing to provide a service on their terms. Some people have the mistaken belief that employers owe them a living. Even if your boss tolerates your idiosyncrasies, this doesn't mean they will choose to promote you in preference to your rivals.

Learning to conform

Most organisations value conformity. Managers tend to establish a good rapport with colleagues who are a 'chip off the old block'. Study those who are successful in the company and those who avoid attracting hassle. Sometimes the lazy individual who does not rock the boat and always agrees with the boss enjoys more latitude than they deserve.

A sales executive who achieves average sales, but is popular with all his peers and never upsets customers, may be a high-flyer in a business that is cultivating a homely image.

Appreciating methodology

The methodology can be more important than outcomes. In some business cultures aggressive marketing, although successful in generating sales, is inconsistent with the image being cultivated and becomes of secondary importance.

A business that values an up-market image, like a city estate agency, may put great store on smart clothing, physical appearance and impeccable manners. On the other hand, market-makers executing deals at the Stock Exchange may place dress sense way down their priority list, their principal concern being that colleagues can work well under extreme pressure and exercise sound judgement.

Evaluating the culture

A business culture exists in each company. To understand this culture address the following questions:

- Who is successful in this company?
- Does the company have any expectations regarding flexible working?
- What is the average working week?
- Are sales executives expected to entertain clients lavishly?
- Is business reliant on the old boys' network?
- Are repeat orders dependent on reciprocal favours or other inducements?
- Does the company follow equal opportunity policies?
- Are ethnic minority groups fairly represented in the workplace?
- Are women's issues fully addressed?
- Does the company pursue a policy of promoting from within?
- Are entrepreneurs and risk-takers valued?

Some of these questions raise ethical issues. Consider whether colleagues have to face difficult ethical dilemmas working for the company.

FACING ETHICAL DILEMMAS AND CONFLICTING LOYALTIES

Some companies put out subtle hidden messages like:

- 'the ends justify the means'
- 'it's all right to cut corners if it increases profits'
- 'if you want to get ahead, join the golf club'
- 'there's no spending limit on entertaining clients providing you get the business.'

Avoiding collusion

Sometimes there is a tacit acceptance of dishonesty, and a blind eye is turned to staff pilfering or fiddling of their expenses:

- 'anything goes provided you are not found out'
- 'they are the perks of the job.'

Shrinkage and wastage

A retail chain which commissioned a firm of management consultants to research to what extent the fall in profits was attributable to 'shrinkage' and 'wastage' found that 60% of all losses were attributable to employee theft. They identified the following abuses:

- discount selling to customers who are friends
- fraudulent refunds to non-existent customers
- key copying, allowing after hours theft to take place
- over-enthusiastic staff who arrive early and leave late
- stock losses from the warehouses.

Whistle-blowing

Many business practices that raise difficult ethical dilemmas for individuals also damage the profitability of the company. If you are shrewd, they can be tackled constructively by making suggestions to senior management that focus on the best interests of the company.

In the example of shrinkage and wastage several suggestions were made to senior management to combat losses and improve profitability:

- Install electronic point of sale (EPOS) systems in all stores, linked by computer to the warehouses/store rooms to monitor all stock movements.

- The use of hidden video cameras and closed-circuit television to monitor store rooms and warehouses 24-hours a day.

- Hire uniformed security staff to detect shoplifters and deter dishonest staff.

- Employ 'honesty shoppers' to look out for signs of leakage in stores.

- Increase audit checks in all stores.

- Instruct supervisors to carry out more frequent checks, including random stock checks.

Using initiative

Most companies reward those who make suggestions which improve the productivity or profitability of the business. Resolve ethical dilemmas profitably without being an obvious whistle-blower.

Confronting issues

Not every ethical dilemma can be tackled this easily. The dilemmas are acute when your boss or colleagues are misappropriating company assets. If you have the courage, collect the necessary evidence and report your concerns to the appropriate manager. It has to be a matter for your conscience and sense of duty.

Resolving dilemmas

Ignoring what is going on around you amounts to collusion. The danger of becoming guilty by association, and the consequent damage to your reputation, is high. Whatever you decide is appropriate in the circumstances, do not under any circumstances take part in any dishonest practice; this leaves you open to prosecution and the sack. It is no defence in law to later claim everyone was involved in the corrupt practice.

SETTING STANDARDS OF CONDUCT

Every company has standards of behaviour which staff are expected to reach, and are set out in its Statement of Values. Your personal credibility depends on being able to answer in the affirmative the following statements about your conduct:

- You act with integrity and are honest.
- You practise and preach equal opportunities.
- You condemn any form of racial or discriminatory behaviour.
- You treat everyone fairly and show no favouritism.
- You do not abuse trust, by fiddling your expense account or by taking unauthorised long lunch breaks.
- You do not make unauthorised long-distance private telephone calls.
- You have never had an office affair.
- You never sexually harass any female colleagues.
- You are completely trustworthy.
- You are not devious or deceitful.
- You are not a political animal.

Building professional credibility

Your colleagues, superiors and bosses expect you to demonstrate evidence of the following professional competencies:

- a natural leader in a crisis;
- someone who is decisive;
- a predictable, consistent and reliable performer;
- an assertive leader who is a problem solver;
- a courageous manager who is prepared to be a risk-taker and meet deadlines;

- a focused, committed, determined and energetic leader;
- an approachable person who is a skilled communicator;
- a charismatic leader who inspires others to turn in their best performance;
- someone with a clear vision and an ideology.

UNDERSTANDING PROFESSIONAL RELATIONSHIPS

Managers have a responsibility to maintain standards of behaviour, lead and empower colleagues. This involves:

- complying with legislative requirements
- dealing with any grievances
- initiating disciplinary action
- maintaining good industrial relations.

Acting professionally

Achieving high standards of behaviour at work means acting in a professional manner. This demands self-discipline, controlling your emotional involvement and maintaining objectivity. A company's code of conduct is undermined when personal feelings are allowed to influence managerial decisions.

Demonstrating leadership

An individual demonstrates qualities of leadership when they:

- have a vision
- communicate clearly
- are supportive and loyal to the team
- develop self-confidence
- give others praise and recognition
- exercise good judgement.

Empowering others

A dynamic and purposeful leader is able to empower others. They achieve this by making a careful and dispassionate assessment of the potential of each team member, identifying any immediate training needs. The next step is to:

- delegate authority to carry out more responsible tasks;
- monitor performance and give constructive feedback;
- offer support and encouragement.

Promoting teamwork

An effective team leader promotes cohesion and harmonious relationships by:

- demonstrating they care about the welfare of colleagues;
- adopting a positive approach;
- maintaining a strong customer focus;
- preventing any form of discriminatory practice from occurring;
- working with the team to achieve their targets.

Motivating the team

A charismatic team leader motivates their team by:

- leading by example
- being energetic
- enthusing others
- encouraging fresh ideas
- being proactive
- remaining calm under pressure
- achieving the goals of the business.

DEVELOPING PERSONAL RELATIONSHIPS

It is normal for friendships to form at work with colleagues. Many people widen their circle of friends at work, which enriches their lives and is beneficial for team-working.

Care needs to be exercised when talking about work in a social setting. Do not discuss personnel issues, as these matters are strictly confidential. Be wary; an accidental leak of 'commercial in confidence' material could damage the company's financial health. Reserve all discussions for the workplace because you can never be sure who may overhear your conversation.

Avoiding problematic areas

Difficulties can arise when friendships form between colleagues of different status at work. Conflicts of interest and divided loyalties can arise, whilst workplace jealousy undermines the unity of the team.

Friendships between a manager and subordinate can be misunderstood and cause difficulties for colleagues. Where there is an unequal balance of power in a relationship, this gives rise to speculation about the following issues:

- Is the manager able to be fair and impartial?

- Will they show favouritism to their friend?

- Where do the loyalties of colleagues lie?

- How will the judgement and credibility of the manager be affected?

Cultivating friendships

Close working relationships can develop quite naturally into friendship outside of work. Friendships between a manager and team members are best avoided if possible. Unless both parties can clearly separate their working roles and responsibilities from their social lives, problems may arise.

Should mistrust develop and the confidence of the team be undermined, such a friendship becomes counter-productive and contrary to the best interests of the company.

Some managers who place themselves in this position, but are keen to maintain their credibility, compensate by being more demanding and expecting higher standards of work from their friends. No friendship between a manager and a colleague who is a poor performer is likely to survive for long. The strain of divided loyalties will force the manager to choose between taking appropriate remedial action or risk being open to the charge of showing favouritism. Once this happens their personal credibility is ruined.

OFFICE AFFAIRS

Romantic liaisons at work are best avoided. The dangers of mixing business and pleasure are well known. It is a lethal cocktail, particularly when the romance occurs between a team member and a member of management. Some companies and organisations forbid such relationships, and if discovered take action to transfer one of the parties involved. This often applies to partners and close family members who are prevented from working in close proximity to each other.

Avoiding serious potential difficulties

Emotional entanglements can be potentially dangerous in certain occupations, like the armed forces and the police. In a business environment it can lead to a wide range of potential problems:

- security breaches and compromises
- irregularities in an audit trail
- collusion in financial matters
- pillow-talk and breaches of confidential information
- resentment and jealousy by colleagues
- suspicion about the motives behind the relationship
- a breakdown in open communication within the team
- colleagues becoming insecure and distrustful, believing everything they say will get back to management
- fear of favouritism
- colleagues feeling embarrassed and awkward in the couple's presence.

Sexual liaisons

Conducting an affair or passionate romance at work makes life difficult for colleagues. Whilst it provides a rich vein of gossip for scandal-mongers, an illicit relationship puts colleagues in the position of having to take sides. Some who strongly disapprove, especially when children are involved, find this can be a source of potential conflict. The worst possible scenario is where the aggrieved partner turns up at work to confront the guilty party or their spouse.

Breaking up

Difficulties arise when an affair or romance comes to an end. A strained atmosphere inevitably develops between the parties, leaving colleagues unsure how to react. Talking about the break-up becomes taboo because everyone feels awkward and doesn't want to get involved or appear to be taking sides. Sooner or later it becomes embarrassing as someone behind with the gossip makes the inevitable *faux pas.*

Handling relationship problems

The business can easily suffer when a relationship ends acrimoniously and love turns into hostility. A scorned boss may become vindictive and try to force a former lover to leave. Sacking someone under these circumstances leaves the company open to an unfair dismissal claim.

Managers need to keep a watchful eye on their staff. **Counselling** should be offered at an early stage if personal problems begin to impact on the productivity of the business. It is legitimate for managers to be concerned about what colleagues get up to at work, or on the company's premises. The social activities and personal lives of colleagues can affect work adversely. The range of problems can be anything from drug dependency and alcohol abuse, to physical or mental illness and emotional problems.

Following the golden rules

The following suggestions are for those colleagues who cannot resist the temptation to get involved with a member of the opposite sex at work:

- Don't discuss your relationship problems at work.

- Don't come to work with new clothes, jewellery or a car; whatever the truth, they will be perceived as presents from your lover.

- Don't give the gossips any ammunition.

HANDLING STRESS WITHIN THE TEAM

Over six million working days are lost each year due to sickness caused by stress. It is becoming an increasing problem for many employees. Everyone faces stress at work, but it is rarely taken seriously until it is too late.

Supporting colleagues

Supporting colleagues who are suffering from the effects of stress calls for sensitivity and an awareness of its behavioural and physical signs. Stress is caused by significant life events or the pressures and demands of an exacting job.

The Working Time Directive

The introduction of the Working Time Directive in 1998 was designed to prevent stress and illness caused by over-work. It gives employees the right to limit their working week to 48 hours, with no individual shift exceeding a maximum of 13 hours. In Great Britain 32% of employees work at least 46 hours a week which compares to an average of 12% throughout the European Union.

Researching stress

The Trade Union Council (TUC) has discovered that loss of self-esteem and lack of control are the most frequent causes of stress amongst their members. Low status, feeling under-valued and lack of feedback from managers all contribute to colleagues feeling under stress. Other research demonstrates that the most stressful events for managers are when they have to make people redundant or take disciplinary action.

Observing physical evidence of stress

Stress affects everyone differently. Some of the physical signs are:

- tiredness

- stomach disorders

- frequent headaches and migraines

- increased smoking and drinking

- mannerisms like twitches, frowning, scowling, or nail-biting

- significant weight loss or gain

- emotional outbursts and tears

- an increase in absenteeism for minor ailments
- low immunity to coughs and colds.

Stress-related sickness

People who appear to have a low immunity to minor ailments may be exhibiting the side-effect of producing excessive amounts of adrenaline, produced when they are under stress. This happens when the body is forced to neglect the body's general maintenance systems to provide energy for 'fight and flight' activities instead.

Identifying behavioural evidence of stress

If you observe a colleague or your boss behaving in the following way you should consider whether they are suffering from stress:

- poor time-keeping and lack of punctuality;
- long lunch-breaks and leaving work early;
- tense and irritable behaviour accompanied by mood swings;
- becoming more withdrawn and less sociable;
- an increase in the number of mistakes they are making;
- poor decision-making and a tendency to procrastinate;
- failing to meet deadlines;
- reduced productivity;
- an increasing level of complaints about poor quality;
- always feeling tired.

Finding sources of support

Good, supportive, trusting working relationships are invaluable. Coping with significant life events or workplace pressures without any emotional support can be very tiring. Sources of emotional support can be any of the following:

- an understanding boss
- family including spouses
- friends

- trusted work colleagues

- counselling from the occupational welfare officer

- advice and guidance from your GP

- professional advice from a solicitor

- self-help books.

The Health and Safety Executive publishes a useful handbook called *Help on Work-Related Stress* which is available free of charge (see Useful Addresses).

Reducing stress levels

Identify what causes you the most frustration and pressure by keeping a stress diary for a few days. This will help you decide whether you need to adjust your lifestyle. Seek inner sources of strength so that you can develop your capacity to cope with stress and pressure. Here are ten tips to combat stress and keep in control:

1. Learn how to relax and consider attending relaxation classes.
2. Develop a healthy lifestyle.
3. Enjoy a balanced diet and keep your weight under control.
4. Take regular daily exercise, join a gynmasium or aerobics class; a recent study revealed that nearly 80% of the most productive workers in a business take regular exercise.
5. Develop a range of relaxing and absorbing interests.
6. Restrict your intake of alcohol and tobacco.
7. Take lunch-breaks, get enough sleep and use all of your holiday entitlement.
8. Stop worrying and learn to think positively.
9. Enjoy life, develop your sense of humour, have regular outings.
10. Nurture a loving relationship with your partner or spouse.

Keeping a sense of perspective

- No one is indispensable.

- No one is irreplaceable.

- No one will thank you if you go sick through stress.

- No one will remember your contribution in 12 months' time!

CASE STUDY

Faye's office affair has repercussions

Fays has channelled her artistic talents into a successful career with the BBC. She is employed as an artistic director in the animation department with the BBC and has broadened her experience by developing the skills of newcomers into the industry.

Faye becomes friendly with Bob, one of her students, and they start a relationship which becomes the talk of the canteen, particularly as both of them are married. Faye has no children, her husband is a businessman in the oil industry and spends many weeks abroad. Bob is married with two pre-school children and considers leaving his wife to live with Faye. Colleagues find the working situation very awkward. Their loyalties are divided, many do not approve of the relationship and this leads to a strained atmosphere within the department. Morale is adversely effected, productivity begins to suffer and deadlines are missed.

Matters eventually come to a head when Faye's husband finds out. There is an ugly scene at work when he confronts Bob and blows are exchanged. A jealous male colleague leaks details of the incident to the press and senior management, who are concerned about adverse publicity and decide to take action. Bob is moved to the Bristol studios and Faye is warned that any further detrimental publicity will result in her being sacked.

Although the relationship cools off over the coming months, things in the department never return to normal. Faye mistrusts her colleagues and harbours resentment towards the colleague she suspects blew the whistle to senior management and the press. Although the gossip eventually subsides, she no longer enjoys the trust and friendship of her colleagues. She eventually decides to leave and now works for another company.

MAKING A PERSONAL ACTION PLAN

1. Make a list of the company's values.

2. Examine whether there are any inconsistencies between these values and the existing business culture.

3. Identify any areas of tension or potential conflict.

4. Do you have a personal relationship at work which causes tension?

5. List all the activities that cause you stress.

6. Devise an action plan to improve your promotion prospects, which addresses the following issues:
   (a) reduces your stress levels by 50%
   (b) improves your compatibility with the company
   (c) enhances your credibility
   (d) improves your promotion prospects.

8

Managing Difficult Situations

HANDLING INTIMIDATION

Any form of prejudice that is evident in the workplace contravenes all equal opportunity policies. Equal opportunities is all about treating people fairly. Racism, sexism, and any form of discrimination against minorities such as those with learning difficulties, physical disabilities or members of the gay community, is unacceptable practice.

A damaging consequence of prejudice is that it leads to discrimination. Victims of discrimination can feel threatened, vulnerable and intimidated, but also angry and frustrated.

Defining terminology

Prejudice
This is when judgements are made about others before an individual has any direct knowledge of them. For example: 'He's a teenager, the last teenager we employed was trouble.'

Stereotyping
This is where a group of individuals is assumed to all share the same negative traits or characteristics. For example: 'All women are bad drivers', 'all black people are lazy.'

Discrimination
This occurs when people act on their prejudices and treat people unfairly without any justification.

Identifying causes of prejudice
Everyone needs to examine their own beliefs, values and attitudes towards minority groups. The usual causes of prejudice in the workplace are:

• ignorance and a lack of awareness;

- the majority feel that the status quo is being challenged;
- cultural influences and upbringing;
- a desire to reflect the views and collude with the power needs of the majority.

Combating prejudice

Prejudice and discrimination can be overcome if colleagues are helped to develop their knowledge base and range of skills. This ignorance can be addressed by:

- developing empathy;
- understanding yourself;
- developing a greater awareness of the needs of others;
- increasing sensitivity to the feelings and opinions of others.

Taking preventative action

The best strategy to use when dealing with any form of prejudice, bullying or harassment in the workplace is to be assertive. Make clear what behaviour is unacceptable and that it should cease immediately. Those who try to ignore offensive behaviour, collude with it, or try to diffuse the situation by joking about it, only make matters worse. Confronting the problem and taking appropriate action is the only way to a satisfactory outcome.

Being assertive and saying no is the first step. Failing that, tell others you have a problem with a particular individual or group of colleagues. Seek support from colleagues, those in management and your union representative.

DEALING WITH SEXUAL HARASSMENT PROBLEMS

Sexual harassment is a form of bullying where the perpetrator, usually a man, acts in a way that the victim finds unacceptable. This mususe of power usually involves picking on a victim who is unlikely to fight back. Sexual harassment can occur in any of the following scenarios:

- The groping boss. A manager who seeks sexual favours in return for preferential treatment or career advancement; the equivalent of the casting couch in the acting profession.

- The male-dominated world. A female with similar qualifications entering a male-dominated environment can pose a threat to male colleagues with fragile egos. They may respond by making her life a misery.

- The female boss. Can be given a difficult time by male colleagues who resent having to take orders from a female manager.

Identifying forms of sexual harassment

Sexual harassment is more common than generally realised. It can occur in any respectable business or organisation. Harassment can include any of the following:

- the use of force to gain sexual favours;

- avoidable, non-accidental touching or brushing up against a colleague;

- customers, colleagues and managers who make sexual propositions to employees;

- offensive and objectional comments about an employee's appearance;

- lewd, degrading and suggestive comments, including remarks about an individual's sexual performance, preferences and orientation;

- staring and leering at colleagues;

- telling embarrassing jokes of a sexual nature;

- displaying scantily clad pin-ups or nude pictures of women (or men) in the workplace.

Emotional pressures

This type of behaviour in the workplace can have a serious and debilitating effect on the individual concerned. Any kind of sexual harassment undermines self-confidence, damages self-esteem, and on an emotional level leaves people feeling anxious and afraid. Any banter, jokes or unwelcome advances that result in colleagues feeling intimidated, humiliated, insulted and victimised must be eliminated.

This behaviour can destroy team morale, reduce productivity and has the potential to end up in an industrial tribunal. This can attract adverse publicity and has associated financial implications.

Understanding the legal position

The main legislation covering sexual harassment are the Sex Discrimination Act, the Employment Protection Act and the Race Relations Act.

The Sex Discrimination Act 1975

This act states that it is illegal to discriminate against anyone because of their gender, or treat them less favourably because they are of a particular sex. An employer can be held responsible for allowing sexual harassment to occur to any of its employees.

The Employment Protection (Consolidated) Act

This legislation provides redress if anyone is sacked or forced to resign as a result of sexual harassment. It allows compensation to be claimed by anyone who has been employed for a minimum period of two years, on the grounds of unfair dismissal.

The Race Relations Act 1976

This act makes it unlawful to discriminate against anyone who is gainfully employed on the grounds of their colour, race, nationality or national ethnic origins.

Taking action

There are several ways to deal with sexual harassment which range from the informal approach to taking formal action. This includes taking legal advice, and in extreme cases taking a grievance to an industrial tribunal. Resolving any problem is further complicated if the victim is of a different ethnic origin, because the sexual harassment often features racism.

The approach to take to resolve this problem is to:

- Inform the person harassing you, either verbally or in writing, to stop.

- Confront the harasser with a friend, colleague or union representative.

- Keep a diary and record every incident and any action you have taken.

- Ask for pin-ups to be removed; if the request is ignored remove them.

- Gather evidence and corroboration of your version of events. This could include secretly recording conversations with the harasser if possible.

- Complain to senior management, your union and seek external advice from the Citizens Advice Bureau and the Equal Opportunities Commission.

- Complain to the police if an indecent assault occurs, as this is a criminal matter.

- Seek legal advice and representation if you have been victimised and have to leave your employment (constructive dismissal) or are sacked (unfair dismissal). You can take your employer to an industrial tribunal for redress and compensation provided you complain within three months from the date of the last incident.

SUPPORTING COLLEAGUES WITH PERSONAL PROBLEMS

Everyone experiences pressure in their lives, but from time to time major life events occur which place us under considerable stress. Major events like illness or injury to family and friends, or the death of a family member, can cause serious distress.

Personal problems, marital difficulties, worries about your children and financial problems affect us all differently. Changing career, fresh employment, moving home, coping with a new addition to the family, are widely recognised as stressful events. They can all have a marked knock-on effect in the workplace which can adversely affect productivity if badly handled.

Analysing significant life events

Two American physicians, Dr Holmes and Dr Rahe, carried out a study to analyse significant life events. They discovered that relationship problems are the most stressful, but even pleasurable events like a welcome addition to the family, coping with Christmas and holidays, make significant demands on our inner resources.

Colleagues who experience serious loss, like the death of a spouse, divorce, separation, imprisonment in the family, injury or illness in the family, and losing their job, are the most vulnerable according to Holmes and Rahe. Their coping resources may be stretched to breaking point. This can lead to illness and in severe cases a complete nervous breakdown.

COPING WITH INDISCIPLINE

We have considered ways that colleagues can experience difficulties in the workplace due to the thoughtless actions of others, or as a consequence of circumstances beyond their control. All managers have a responsibility to deal with personnel problems in a sensitive way, but to confront individuals whose behaviour is unacceptable. Most companies set out their disciplinary procedures in a code of conduct and discipline which makes clear what standards of behaviour are expected at work. It should specify how any instances of misconduct are to be handled.

The informal approach

The main aim of a line manager when faced with indiscipline is to maintain control and make sure the set standards of conduct are upheld. The emphasis with the individual concerned is to encourage them to improve their behaviour and attitude. Counselling and informal guidance should be used wherever possible, with formal action taken if no improvement results from this approach. Sometimes there is no alternative to formal action if a serious breach of discipline has occurred, like theft or fraud at the workplace.

The focus of any disciplinary action should be to ensure compliance with acceptable standards of conduct. It is not intended to be a means of punishing an individual or seeking retribution.

Handling disciplinary matters

Line managers are responsible for maintaining discipline amongst their colleagues. They must act objectively and reasonably, taking care not to discriminate against any individual or particular group. If disciplinary action should prove necessary there should not be any avoidable delay. The guiding principle should be *justice delayed is justice denied*. The timetable for action normally agreed with staff representatives, and set out in the code of conduct, should be followed.

Principles of natural justice
The rules of natural justice should govern any disciplinary action, and be handled with discretion and in confidence.

- The employee is advised of the case against them.

- They are allowed to state their case and challenge the evidence presented.

- Any witnesses for the defence are invited to attend.

- The employee is allowed to have assistance in the form of a colleague or trade union representative.

- The standard of proof required is 'the balance of probabilities', but is tempered by the need to be a good employer, and be 'fair and reasonable'.

- Proven misconduct results in consistent and predictable penalties. The penalties should range from a formal oral, written and final warning, to financial restitution and ultimately dismissal. Although dismissal is not normally for a first offence, serious misconduct like a serious act of negligence resulting in significant loss to the company can result in dismissal.

- There is a right of appeal in all cases.

UNDERSTANDING THE NEEDS OF COLLEAGUES WITH DISABILITIES

Disability is still a serious problem in the workplace, although considerable progress has been achieved in recent years. Appreciating the problems facing a colleague with a disability demands sensitivity. Some people unwittingly display prejudice, are ignorant about their needs and discriminate against those with disabilities. This insensitivity can take several forms:

- using inappropriate language

- being patronising

- being over-helpful

- showing pity

- emphasising the differences between able-bodied and colleagues with disabilities.

Addressing the legal position
There are several pieces of legislation which address the needs of those with disabilities:

- The Disabled Persons Employment Act 1944
- The Disabled Persons Act 1981
- Equal Pay Act 1970
- Equal Pay (Amendment) Act 1983
- The Disability Discrimination Act.

All this legislation is designed to create a fair and just society. It aims to promote conditions which foster equality of treatment by:

- setting up a register of disabled persons;
- obliging employers to employ a quota of people with disabilities;
- reserving certain occupations for those with disabilities;
- eliminating discrimination between men and women on pay;
- establishing the principle of equal pay for equal work;
- making workplace discrimination unlawful in businesses with fewer than 15 employees.

The disabling environment
Colleagues with a disability often find their physical disability is less of a handicap than the **disabling environment**, as this restricts their ability to be independent. Disabled employees who are wheelchair-bound often have to contend with additional obstacles in the workplace:

- problems of access to buildings
- a lack of ramps for their wheelchair
- narrow corridors and impassable doors
- no lifts

- lack of suitable facilities

- wash-basins and towel rails which are too high to reach

- inaccessible toilets.

Working with blind and partially sighted colleagues

According to the Royal National Institute for the Blind about 75% of blind people are unemployed, which is a higher level than for ex-offenders. The main issues of concern to the blind or partially sighted are:

- people who shout at those who are partially sighted, and assume they are also hard of hearing;

- obstacles in the workplace, like machinery, equipment, office furniture;

- trailing telephone wires and electrical cables;

- thoughtless colleagues who rearrange office furniture or equipment without forewarning them.

Working with deaf and hard of hearing colleagues

Colleagues who take the trouble to learn sign language or to finger-spell have a distinct advantage. The British Sign Language is recommended for finger-spelling. Fortunately most deaf persons are adept at lip-reading. Communicating with the deaf is much easier if colleagues:

- face the deaf person, as this helps them to lip-read;

- speak clearly, and try to avoid technical language and complex words where possible;

- appreciate deaf colleagues feel sensitive about:
  (a) being unable to join in a conversation easily
  (b) feeling an outsider
  (c) other colleagues talking about them or making jokes at their expense.

Coping with disabilities

The potential for problems in the workplace with a disabled colleague is greatly reduced if there is open and sympathetic discussion about their needs. In the case of blind and deaf colleagues they often know what technical help is available to assist them. Catering for the needs of wheelchair users may involve the employer making some structural alterations, although financial assistance may be available from the local authority. Some modifications may simply involve lowering shelves and rearranging furniture, whilst reallocating certain tasks like photocopying to other colleagues may be a sensible option.

There are encouraging signs that life will become easier for the disabled in the workplace as the law becomes better understood and advances in technology ease practical problems.

There are plans to introduce a Disability Rights Commission to assist and represent disabled people who experience discrimination in the workplace.

AVOIDING MISUNDERSTANDINGS

An ex-offender is under a legal obligation to tell a prospective employer about any convictions they have if asked, unless these are **spent**.

The Rehabilitation of Offenders Act 1974

This legislation allows offenders legally to forget a criminal conviction after a **rehabilitation period**. This helps to counter prejudice against ex-offenders which can nullify all their efforts to make a fresh start. The length of the rehabilitative period directly relates to the length of sentence and not the time actually spent in custody. In the case of a sentence of two-and-a-half years or more it never becomes *spent* (see Figure 10).

Disclosing previous convictions

There are a number of exceptions to the Rehabilitation of Offenders Act where previous convictions must be disclosed:

- Applications to join certain professions where legal protection applies, including accountants, chemists, dentists, doctors, lawyers and nurses.

- Appointments to certain sensitive occupations which give access to children and youngsters under the age of 18. This includes childminders, foster parents, prison officers, the police, probation officers, school caretakers, social workers, teachers, traffic wardens and youth workers.

Sentence	Rehabilitation period	
	Over 17 on conviction	*Under 17 on conviction*
Prison or Youth Custody of more than 6 months and less than 2½ years	10 years	5 years
Prison or Youth Custody of less than 6 months	7 years	3½ years
Fine or Community Order	5 years	2½ years
Absolute Discharge	6 months	3 months
Probation, Supervision, Care Order, Conditional Discharge or Bind-Over	1 year, or until the order expires, whichever is the longer	
Attendance Centre Order	1 year after the order expires	
Hospital Orders with or without a restriction order	5 years, or 2 years after the order expires, whichever is the longer	

Fig. 10. The Rehabilitation of Offenders Act 1974.

- Certain regulated occupations, including casino operators, directors and managers of insurance companies and unit trusts, firearms dealers and nursing home proprietors.

- Appointments to jobs where national security could be compromised, including certain posts in the civil service and defence contractors.

- Applications for firearms certificates, shotguns or explosives.

Applying for work
When applying for a job ex-offenders are entitled to answer no to any question on the application form or at interview that refers

to a spent conviction, provided the job in question is not exempt from the Act. An untruthful answer to a question that refers to unspent convictions can lead to possible prosecution. Obtaining a job by deceiving an employer is also grounds for instant dismissal.

The period of rehabilitation that applies under the Act depends on how old the offender is on conviction. If he or she was convicted under the age of 17, a shorter period of rehabilitation is applicable.

Seeking help

Agencies like the Apex Trust offer help, advice and guidance with employment problems. They publish literature encouraging employers to pursue equal opportunity policies and not discriminate against ex-offenders. They have offices throughout the country but can be contacted through their headquarters (see Useful Addresses).

SELF-APPRAISAL

Dealing with personnel issues and difficult situations is an inescapable part of being a manager. Some problems result from inappropriate behaviour but others concern colleagues needing help with personal difficulties.

The welfare of your staff should be a priority. Most personal crises can be prevented, and productivity maintained, by timely action. No one can perform efficiently if they are struggling with insurmountable work or personal problems. Every manager needs to develop their interpersonal and counselling skills, to equip them to handle sensitive issues confidently.

Appraising yourself

1. Do you have good counselling skills?

	Yes	No	Sometimes
(a) You always see colleagues whenever they ask to see you.			
(b) Your standard response to a colleague with a problem is 'That happened to me once, let me share my experience with you.'			

	Yes	No	Sometimes
(c) Asking open-ended questions is your speciality.			
(d) You like giving advice to colleagues, it makes you feel superior to them.			
(e) You try to encourage people to come up with their own solution to a problem.			
(f) You believe in strict confidentiality when counselling someone.			
(g) Colleagues suffering with stress can be easily identified.			

2. Are you confident about handling difficult situations?

(a) When faced with having to make someone redundant you try to be sociable before breaking the bad news to them.

(b) You are open, direct and firm with people.

(c) 'I will give you an explanation, but I am not going to argue with you' is your approach.

(d) You believe it is important to explain clearly a person's entitlements on leaving your employment.

(e) It is always appropriate to offer counselling.

(f) The company car must always be returned immediately someone loses their job.

(g) You do not consider it is your place, or appropriate, to offer advice about finding another job to someone you have dismissed.

(h) Sensitivity and tact are the most important skills to develop.

	Yes	No	Sometimes

3. Are you good at investigating problems?

(a) You always listen to any explanations before deciding what action to take.

(b) You feel uncomfortable if you are not in charge of every situation.

(c) You complete the answer to a question for a colleague when they are slow in answering.

(d) You are always keen to establish the facts.

(e) You find being provocative encourages people to tell you what you need to know.

(f) When you are unsure about the solution to a problem you cover by asking lots of intelligent questions.

(g) You think it is clever when you are in an awkward spot to answer a question with one of your own.

(h) You never let people know what you are really feeling, or show any emotion.

4. Are you a problem-solver?

(a) You adopt a systematic approach to solving problems.

(b) 'The real problem is not the presenting problem.'

(c) Most problems are insoluble, you can only treat the symptoms.

(d) Generating a range of possible solutions is the best way you know to solve a problem.

(e) There is often more than one solution to a problem.

(f) Experience is invaluable when dealing with personnel problems.

	Yes	No	Sometimes
(g) You believe brainstorming is an effective way to generate ideas and solutions to problems.			
(h) Conducting a SWOT analysis is a useful technique which encourages participation.			

5. Are you a wise leader?

(a) You are open about your business plans with the rest of the team.			
(b) You always avoid giving any negative feedback.			
(c) You concentrate on developing the strengths of team members.			
(d) 'Everyone thrives on praise.'			
(e) 'Criticise publicly and give praise in private.'			
(f) You are never hard on a colleague who is feeling down.			
(g) Recognition is more important than a pay rise based on merit.			
(h) If anyone has a good idea you always give them the credit.			
(i) You always take the blame when things go wrong.			
(j) 'When I delegate responsibility, I don't always delegate authority.'			
(k) 'I always practise what I preach, and try to be a good role model.'			

How did you score?

1. Do you have good counselling skills?

	Yes	No	Sometimes
(a)	3	0	2
(b)	0	3	1
(c)	3	0	1
(d)	0	3	1
(e)	3	1	2

(f)	3	0	1
(g)	2	1	3

Maximum score: 21 Average score: 10 Unacceptable score: 5

2. Are you confident about handling difficult situations?

	Yes	**No**	**Sometimes**
(a)	0	3	1
(b)	2	0	3
(c)	3	0	1
(d)	2	0	3
(e)	2	1	3
(f)	1	3	2
(g)	1	3	2
(h)	3	0	1

Maximum score: 24 Average score: 13 Unacceptable score: 6

3. Are you good at investigating problems?

	Yes	**No**	**Sometimes**
(a)	3	0	1
(b)	1	3	3
(c)	0	3	1
(d)	3	0	1
(e)	0	3	1
(f)	0	3	1
(g)	1	3	2
(h)	1	3	2

Maximum score: 24 Average score: 11 Unacceptable score: 5

4. Are you a problem-solver?

	Yes	**No**	**Sometimes**
(a)	3	0	1
(b)	2	1	3
(c)	0	3	2
(d)	3	0	1
(e)	3	0	1
(f)	3	1	2
(g)	3	0	2
(h)	3	0	2

Maximum score: 24 Average score: 13 Unacceptable score: 6

5. Are you a wise leader?

	Yes	No	Sometimes
(a)	3	0	2
(b)	0	3	1
(c)	3	0	1
(d)	3	0	1
(e)	0	3	1
(f)	3	0	1
(g)	0	3	1
(h)	3	0	0
(i)	3	0	1
(j)	0	3	0
(k)	3	0	1

Maximum score: 33 Average score: 16 Unacceptable score: 8

MAKING A PERSONAL ACTION PLAN

1. Attend a course on equal opportunities training.

2. Ensure you are up to date with the major employment law changes.

3. Observe a case at an industrial tribunal as a learning experience.

4. Keep a stress diary for a few days and identify the main sources of stress for you at work.

5. Devise a personal stress reduction strategy.

6. Ask your line manager and a colleague for feedback on how well you cope with stress.

9

Achieving Your Ambitions

DEMONSTRATING YOUR POTENTIAL

Working for a successful organisation or company is a sound method of achieving your ambitions, as it allows you opportunities to demonstrate your talents. A successful company is productive, efficient and produces goods of high quality with a minimum amount of time spent rectifying faults. It reduces overheads and increases profitability by enthusing its staff, being receptive to new ideas, recognising and developing the potential of managers and the workforce alike.

Being aware of Investors in People

Currently 11,000 organisations have achieved the Investors in People standard, and another 21,000 are committed to attaining the standard. Altogether 7.7 million people, or 34% of the total workforce, are working in organisations and companies which see the advantages of investing in their staff. By allocating resources to training which develops their skills, companies improve their productivity, their profitability, reduce sickness and absenteeism and improve morale.

A wide range of companies and organisations in the public and private sectors have achieved the Standard. They include British Steel, De Vere Hotels, Elida Faberge, Bradford & Bingley Building Society, and Warrington Hospital (NHS) Trust. The government has produced a White Paper *Development and Training for Civil Servants* which commits it to achieving the Standard for all civil servants by the year 2000.

Understanding the role of the TEC

The Training and Enterprise Councils (TECs), or Local Enterprise Companies (LECs) as they are known in Scotland, have an important role to play in the Investors in People initiative. Their role is to encourage employers to invest in improving the skills of their staff. An important role of the local TEC is to encourage companies and organisations to achieve the Investors in People

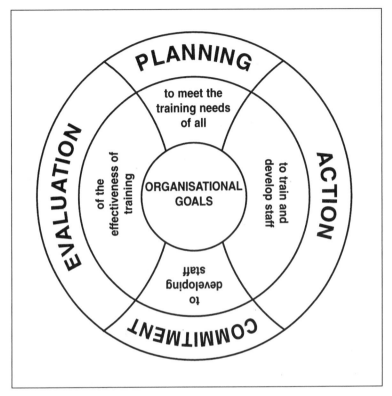

Fig. 11. The Investors in People principles.

Standard and play an active part in the process and issuing the Certificate of Commitment to companies who sign up and submit an agreed action plan.

INVESTING IN PEOPLE

Investors in People is training and developing the skills of all staff so that they improve their performance and achieve the goals of the business (see Figure 11).

Using the PACE approach
Four principles underpin the Investors in People (IiP) Standard, easily recalled by the word PACE:

- **P**lanning
- **A**ction
- **C**ommitment
- **E**valuation.

Regular planning

The training and development of staff needs to be carried out in a **planned** way with regular reviews of progress. The written **action plan** should clearly set out the company's goals and targets, identify the training and development needs and provide the necessary resources. Responsibility for the overall training programme should be clearly established. All training provided should be accredited and linked to national standards like National Vocational Qualifications (NVQs) or Scottish Vocational Qualifications (SVQs).

Taking effective action

Managers are proactive and take **action** to meet identified training needs in a planned way. This begins with an effective **induction** programme and continues with an ongoing process of **job-related training**. Managers throughout the company take effective action to discharge their responsibilities, and ensure all training and developmental needs are addressed.

Demonstrating management commitment

There must be a demonstrable **commitment** by management to develop people and improve their overall performance. This message has to be communicated throughout the company. Everyone needs to be aware of the vision and goals of the business and to have an opportunity to contribute to its success.

Measuring and evaluating

A proper **evaluation** of the effectiveness of training provided should be carried out to assess its impact on the company's performance. The relationship between the investment by management in training and development has to be carefully assessed so that it can be demonstrated to be cost-effective and value for money.

TAKING THE LONG-TERM VIEW

A successful company appreciates its staff and values their contribution. It has developed a culture of teamwork which permeates from the boardroom to the shop-floor. By concentrating on meeting the needs of its staff the company is able to keep its customers satisfied and maintain a competitive edge.

The far-sighted company will give high priority to investing heavily in training and developing the potential of all its staff. There are benefits from this approach for:

- every member of staff

- the company

- the customers.

Developing the potential of staff

Each member of the team benefits by:

- increased job satisfaction

- having their achievements recognised

- receiving training in a planned way

- having a sense of pride that comes from working for a successful company.

Benefiting the company

The company or organisation benefits from having a trained and highly skilled workforce in the following ways:

- having a highly motivated workforce

- higher productivity

- improved efficiency

- a loyal and satisfied customer base

- increased profits and dividends for the shareholders.

Improving customer focus

Customers benefit considerably when the company focus is on customer care:

- high levels of customer satisfaction
- customers feel they receive good value for money
- good after-sales service
- brand loyalty
- their confidence in the quality of the products the company are offering leads to repeat business.

The contribution of IiP

Companies which achieve the IiP Standard to develop their staff report the following benefits:

- Managers are more focused and concentrate on the important issues.

- The staff are aware of the company's plans and goals.

- The culture changes to one where the emphasis is on meeting customer needs.

- Everyone feels valued in the company, and energy levels, enthusiasm, cohesion and commitment increase.

- Stress levels reduce as colleagues and managers become more relaxed.

- Relationships improve, people display a good sense of humour (one of the first casualties of high stress levels).

- Improved levels of self-confidence are evident.

ADDRESSING IDENTIFIED WEAKNESSES

The Investors in People process is designed to achieve quality work and get the best from everybody in the company. This process provides the framework for conducting appraisals on all staff, enabling feedback and identifying strengths and weaknesses (see Figure 12). The aim is to improve the performance of everyone and identify whether further training will enhance performance.

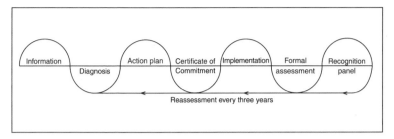

Fig. 12. The Investors in People process

The Investors in People process

1. Information
Information about the Standard is obtained from the local Training Enterprise Council (TEC) or Local Enterprise Company (LEC) in Scotland.

2. Diagnosis
An initial diagnosis is made against the Standard using the services of the local TEC/LEC.

3. Action plan
The senior management team devises an action plan to remedy shortcomings identified in the diagnosis.

4. Certificate of Commitment
The local TEC/LEC endorses the action plan and issues a Certificate of Commitment.

5. Implementation
The action plan is successfully carried out.

6. Formal assessment
This is carried out by an independent assessor who examines a portfolio of evidence and interviews a representative group of staff.

7. Recognition panel
Once the assessor is satisfied the company meets the Standard, the report is submitted to an independent recognition panel who award Investor in People accreditation.

8. Reassessment every three years
The award lasts for three years, then the process is repeated because continuous improvement is an integral part of the Standard.

CARRYING OUT A STAFF APPRAISAL

A staff appraisal is an opportunity to sit down with your line manager to review your performance and receive feedback. The review should compare your performance against agreed targets set at the beginning of the year. Some of the topics to discuss are:

- how well you are performing;
- your ability to achieve the company's targets;
- whether you are living up to your boss's expectations;
- how well you work with other team members;
- any concerns about your attitude;
- identifiable training needs;
- your professional and career goals.

Achieving quality work

It is essential that all members of the team are working together in harmony, and that everyone is clear about their role and responsibilities. Before the line manager conducting the staff appraisal can assess a team member's performance, they should satisfy themselves that the postholder has:

- a job description which sets down the main responsibilities and quality standard expected;
- been allocated the agreed level of resources;
- the opportunity to gauge how well they are performing their duties;
- received training in the relevant procedures and systems;
- access to advice and guidance;
- been offered direction, support and encouragement.

Checking the job description

Every employee must be given a clear **job description** which lists the main duties and responsibilities of the postholder. The job description normally follows this format:

- **Job title.**

- **Job purpose.** Summarises the scope of the responsibilities.

- **Accountability**: Identifies the line manager.

- **Resources**. Lists the staff, buildings, equipment and services they manage.

- **List of responsibilities**. The main duties and performance criteria are listed:
  (a) the standard of service delivery or performance required
  (b) the budgetary constraints
  (c) their personnel duties.

- **Cover arrangements**. Identifies how any absences are covered.

- **Performance criteria**. This states the methodology used to judge overall performance. The performance criteria may be expressed in financial terms, or the level of sales, or the volume of production expected.

A competency-based model

Many companies and organisations have a competency-based approach which incorporates into the job description the **core competencies** necessary to perform the job effectively. These identifiable essential skills can vary enormously, but the following is an example of the core competencies which a manager needs to possess:

- systematic and procedural skills

- planning and reviewing

- organising and empowering

- interpersonal skills

- motivation and commitment

- communication skills

- problem-solving ability

- commitment to continuous improvement

- leadership and decision-making ability

- team-building and networking skills

- negotiating ability

- technical and professional expertise

- ability to manage change.

Setting objectives
Best practice is to plan and agree the **objectives** at the beginning of the year. The golden rule for setting objectives is to make them SMART:

- **S**pecific

- **M**easurable

- **A**chievable

- **R**ealistic

- **T**imebound.

Mid-way during the year formally review progress. Check whether any changes have occurred which make the objectives unachievable or superfluous, and revise them accordingly.

At the end of the year check out the level of performance achieved in relation to the objectives set, then arrange a staff appraisal interview.

REVIEWING PERFORMANCE

There are four essential components to a successful staff appraisal interview:

- **Confidential discussion**. It must be a two-way process which involves sharing information, giving positive feedback and making constructive criticism.

- **Factually based**. All feedback should be factually based and capable of being supported by examples. Avoid being subjective or forming an opinion based on gossip, as this is counter-productive.

- **Be realistic**. Concentrate on areas of performance that can be improved through further training or increased effort. Do not criticise personality traits as they cannot be changed.

- **Be honest**. Be open and honest. Do not skirt around problem areas or fudge issues by using jargon. Discuss problem areas openly, but with tact and sensitivity.

Ensuring a successful outcome

The template that follows can assure a successful outcome, providing you approach the interview constructively, allocate sufficient time to discuss issues thoroughly and ensure there are no interruptions.

1. Prepare beforehand.
2. Put them at their ease.
3. Explain the process.
4. Discuss the objectives set at the last appraisal.
5. Encourage them to contribute.
6. Identify problems beyond the postholder's control.
7. Consider the adequacy of available resources.
8. Set fresh objectives consistent with the company's goals.
9. Identify any training and developmental needs.
10. Prepare an action plan which enhances their career prospects.

Changing behaviour

Conducting a staff appraisal is the first stage in encouraging a colleague to modify their behaviour. Constructive and honest feedback allows the individual to address shortcomings, and adjust their behaviour or attitude accordingly. Where the required quality standard is not being met the focus may be on individual or team training needs.

A team member's behaviour can be positively influenced by demonstrating you care about them and value their contribution. Emphasise the importance of teamwork and appeal to their natural desire not to let the team down. Build their self-esteem and self-confidence. The purpose of the staff appraisal is to improve the individual's performance and the effectiveness of the whole team. It is essential to:

- set clear goals
- ensure everyone is pulling in the same direction
- identify what motivates the individual.

REWARDING GOOD PERFORMANCE

The hierarchy of needs theory, devised by Maslow, identifies that higher level needs people strive to meet the needs of self-esteem and self-actualisation. In practice, every ambitious person trying to progress their career has different plans:

- Some want to improve their professional skills and reputation.
- Others want to move up the corporate ladder within the company.
- A few may see their future prospects with another company.

Analysing ingredients of success

Career success is usually inextricably linked to the fortunes of the company. Gaining recognition and achieving career goals means making yourself visible. Working for a company that believes in promoting from within provides more opportunities to make a positive impact with senior managers. However, a serious mistake can destroy your future prospects within the company.

Building a personal profile

Identify the personal qualities and attributes that set you apart from your colleagues:

- **Drive**. A focused person with a strong desire to achieve targets.
- **Energy**. Someone who is lively and always gives 100% effort.
- **Determination**. A resilient person who is not deflected from achieving objectives by opposition, difficulties and setbacks.
- **Persistence**. Someone who has the stamina to persevere.
- **Motivation**. The driving force for wanting to do something, like accepting a challenge.

- **Charisma**. A charismatic leader is someone with a strong personality who inspires and motivates others.

Developing a professional reputation

A good professional reputation is highly prized. It is achieved by developing a level of skill and expertise that makes you in demand and gains you the respect of colleagues:

Professional integrity
An honest individual, who takes full responsibility for their actions and always acts in the best interests of the company.

Reliability
Someone who is dependable and a safe pair of hands who keeps line management informed.

Professional pride
A meticulous, careful person who takes trouble to get the facts and details right (not to be confused with arrogant or conceited).

Analytical ability
Someone with good reasoning skills who is able to absorb a large quantity of complex data.

Communication skills
The ability to get the message across clearly, succinctly and persuasively, verbally or in writing.

Listening skills
A person who listens attentively to what others have to say.

Having a record of achievement

Anyone wishing to convince their boss of their readiness to handle greater responsibility should compile a portfolio of their achievements. Every company is primarily interested in making money, so demonstrate ways you have improved productivity or efficiency. This could be by suggesting ways to streamline procedures or reduce wastage of time and money.

Gaining recognition

If you have outstanding personal qualities, professional expertise and a record of solid achievement, you are invaluable. Make sure your contribution to the success of the business is recognised and reflected in your annual staff appraisal. Convince your boss, and it can only be a question of time before you gain the promotion and recognition you richly deserve.

Getting promoted
Once promotion arrives, don't believe all your own publicity. Don't forget:

- Pride comes before a fall.

- Some colleagues will be delighted to see you fail.

- Managers are monitoring how you handle increased responsibility.

Be sensitive to the feelings of colleagues who have been disappointed, some may feel jealous or aggrieved. Take care not to give anyone an opportunity to undermine your position or damage your credibility.

HANDLING SETBACKS

Life is about taking risks, learning to cope with failure and rejection. A successful salesperson quickly develops a thick skin, as rejection goes with the territory.

Being turned down for promotion within the company can be painful and damaging to your self-esteem, if handled incorrectly. It is particularly disappointing if your most recent staff appraisal highlights your potential, and demonstrates you achieved all the objectives set by the company.

Setbacks are a stern test of character. The ability to take knocks and bounce back is part of working life. It builds character, and may make you an understanding and tolerant boss.

The key to success is to adopt the right attitude and be persistent. No one expects to succeed every time. William Edward Hickson, a British educationalist, said: 'If at first you don't succeed, try, try again.'

Avoiding mistakes
A colleague who cannot take constructive criticism invariably becomes bitter and cynical when they fail to get promoted. The

underlying problem is they are insecure and lack self-confidence. This results in their pride and self-esteem being irreparably damaged when they encounter rejection so they need to find a scapegoat.

They should consider what lessons can be learnt for next time, like improving their interviewing technique. Instead they complain loudly about the incompetence and lack of integrity of the interviewing panel. A few advertise their immaturity, poor judgement and unsuitability for promotion by making a formal complaint.

Acting maturely

Seek feedback about your recent performance and discuss with your line manager how you can do better next time. Signal your willingness to learn from experience, and make it clear it is your intention to continue serving the company to the best of your ability.

MAKING A PERSONAL ACTION PLAN

1. Identify your key personal qualities and attributes.

2. Make a list of your professional skills.

3. Outline your main achievements in the past 12 months.

4. Check the completed staff appraisal does justice to your full range of qualities, skills and achievements.

5. Identify areas for improvement with your line manager:
   (a) skill deficiencies
   (b) problem areas
   (c) developmental areas.

6. Incorporate areas you have identified where there is room for improvement as targets in next year's staff appraisal.

10

A Winning Formula

WORKING FOR A WINNER

Everyone wants to be part of a winning team where enthusiasm, motivation and self-belief are high. In a successful team colleagues are keen to support and co-operate with each other. Leaders of winning teams make sure everyone's efforts are channelled profitably into maximising output and achieving high standards.

Recognising a winning boss

You have found a winning boss if there is evidence of the following skills:

(a) They are a good communicator with well developed listening skills, receptive to new ideas and an innovator.
(b) They are supportive and stimulate the team to achieve their targets.
(c) They show a high level of concern for the welfare of the team.
(d) They set high standards and expect team members to achieve them.
(e) Their professional knowledge base is extensive and they challenge the team to be the best.
(f) They are willing to delegate.
(g) They adopt a participative style of management and treat you as an equal.
(h) They appreciate your best efforts and give honest, constructive feedback.

If your boss measures up to this specification, then you are working for a winner!

WINNING RELATIONSHIPS

Good relationships lie at the heart of effective team-working. A team that works together harmoniously, and relates positively to their boss and other colleagues, has developed good interpersonal skills.

Avoiding poor relationships

A lack of enthusiasm, poor motivation, paranoia and high stress levels are all indicative of unhealthy working relationships. Other symptons of poor relationships are:

- **Distrust**. An avoidance of sharing and exchanging information.

- **Hostility**. Personality clashes between team members which result in frequent arguments, friction and tension.

- **Conflict**. Jealousy and intense rivalry between team members, resulting in obstructive behaviour, impedes the decision-making process.

- **Confrontation**. A hostile, destructive working environment, where aggressive behaviour is tolerated, discourages the more passive, quieter team members from contributing.

Promoting good relationships

Good relationships flourish in an environment that values:

- **Openness**. Freedom of speech is positively welcomed.

- **Trust**. Honest relationships based on mutual respect where confidentiality is respected.

- **Participation**. A consultative approach, which involves team members in the decision-making process, engenders ownership in agreed outcomes.

- **Mutual support**. A culture of reciprocal support, where training and supervision is promoted.

- **Co-operation**. Team-building is fostered through open communication and honest feedback, in order to achieve team goals.

ANALYSING RELATIONSHIPS

A useful tool which describes how people relate to each other is **transactional analysis**. This theory, devised by Eric Berne, identifies three principal roles individuals adopt when relating to work colleagues.

The parent role

The **parental role** sets standards, makes the rules and sets boundaries.

Someone adopting a **critical parent** role makes judgements, criticises others and is full of their own self-importance.

A **nurturing parent** role is adopted by someone who finds satisfaction in caring for or protecting others. The nurturing parent can also be dominant, over-protective and possessive.

The adult role

Team members who consistently adopt an **adult role** should always be your first choice, as they take a constructive and positive approach. They tend to be rational, calm, confident, thoughtful and flexible. They have the ability to question issues, be analytical, think laterally and plan effectively.

The child role

The **child role** varies enormously. It can be used to describe spontaneous, creative behaviour, and behaviour that is manipulative and immature.

The **natural child** is uninhibited, outspoken, imaginative, creative, fun-loving, carefree, adventurous and affectionate.

The **adapted child** is negative, defiant, angry, rebellious and constantly grumbles. They can also be meek, submissive, repressed, over-conforming and lacking in initiative.

The **manipulative child** is selfish, self-centred and highly political. They use charm and inter-personal skills to indulge egotistical behaviour.

Transactional analysis

Analysing relationships within a team can be achieved using transactional analysis. The ideal situation is one where adult to adult relationships are the norm, and rational, mature behaviour is the outcome.

Colleagues and bosses, deliberately or subconsciously, adopt a variety of different roles depending on the circumstances. For instance, the nurturing parent is very supportive to the child when assistance, help and encouragement are needed. They respond in nurturing mode when setbacks or mistakes occur.

In a company where a blame culture exists, the critical parent is often in evidence. They seek to avoid responsibility when things go wrong, and blame the staff if production or sales targets are not met.

Games people play

Four main types of interaction can be observed (see Figure 13):

Adult to adult
This is the ideal type of interaction to have within the team. It is based on rational argument and discussion, conducted openly and honestly.

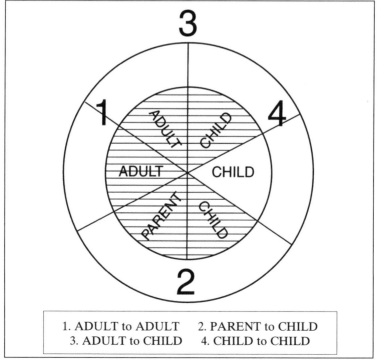

Fig. 13. Games people play.

Parent to child
The nurturing parent encourages the child by showing under-standing, offering support and setting boundaries.

Adult to child
In this role-play the adult may project blame, be patronising or adopt a dominant approach. This can stifle the use of initiative and suppress a full and open exchange of views.

Child to child
This is characterised by argumentative behaviour, squabbling and malicious gossip. At its best it can be creative, with fun, laughter, practical jokes and wacky ideas in abundance.

Making observations
Analyse how your boss, colleagues and team members relate to each other. Observe how they cope with problems, setbacks and stress:

- Do they adopt different roles from the normal adult mode?

- Are some colleagues locked into playing a certain role at work?

- Do some colleagues meet their need for power, support and attention by adopting certain roles within the team?

CARING FOR COLLEAGUES

Human beings are not machines. Everyone has a distinct personality with emotional, social, intellectual and psychological requirements that need satisfying if they are to function effectively. Significant life events and crises can prevent your undivided attention being focused on the needs of the company.

Being human
Colleagues experiencing health problems need to be encouraged to see their own doctor at an early stage, particularly if they are under extreme stress, or have a drink or drug related problem. Anyone with personal or domestic problems should contact the staff welfare officer for confidential advice or counselling.

Tender loving care

When facing difficulties in our personal lives, it is easier to cope if your colleagues and boss are sympathetic and understanding. No one knows when tragedy or disaster may strike them. We live our lives pretending we are invincible and immortal, in the fond belief that we are somehow different from everyone else. Caring for colleagues should be an integral part of every company that means business about Investing in People.

Available assistance

Many companies have a wide range of services available for their employees. A large national company should be able to offer the following benefits:

- special leave
- advance of pay
- child care facilities
- career breaks
- compassionate transfers
- counselling services.

Taking special leave

Staff can apply for special paid leave when a domestic problem or crisis arises, to help them make short-term arrangements. The problem can range from a fire, flood, or burglary at home, to being embroiled in a matrimonial dispute and arranging care for elderly relatives. Special leave is often approved for occasions like:

(a) marriage
(b) maternity or paternity leave
(c) ante-natal appointments
(d) to provide care for a close relative who is seriously ill
(e) the death of a close relative, spouse or child
(f) a course of study leading to a recognised vocational, technical or managerial qualification.

Receiving financial assistance

Some companies provide packages of financial assistance in the form of loans:

(a) to purchase a season ticket
(b) for an annual car parking ticket
(c) at Christmas
(d) towards the cost of moving house.

Providing child care facilities

Many companies provide their own crèche or nursery facilities for working colleagues with child care responsibilities. They also may have a range of flexible working arrangements which are tailored to the domestic needs of their staff. These may include:

- flexible working hours schemes

- job share arrangements

- career breaks.

Taking a career break

A career break can enable a colleague to take extended unpaid leave for up to five years, in order to care for young children or elderly relatives. At the end of this period they can return to the company and resume their career.

Compassionate transfers

A large company has the scope and resources to assist transfer to another branch of the business:

- on health grounds

- for compassionate reasons

- for domestic reasons.

Relocating employees

Most companies meet relocation costs when someone is promoted or compulsorily transferred. A transfer in the best interests of the company can involve moving house, disrupting the children's education and uprooting the family by taking them away from relatives and friends.

The best interests of the company are always served by dealing considerately and sensitively with key workers, because moving house is a stressful experience for the whole family.

COUNSELLING COLLEAGUES

Counselling is a professional service provided by some companies. Counsellors help colleagues with personal and domestic difficulties by allowing them to verbalise their thoughts and feelings, and come to terms with painful situations like the break-up of a marriage or a family bereavement.

How counselling helps
Many people facing personal problems respond positively to counselling. The most difficult step is acknowledging there is a problem, and asking for help. Colleagues experiencing the following problems are likely to benefit from counselling:

- feeling they are not coping
- unsure how to tackle a problem
- feeling unwanted and alone
- unable to sleep through worry
- eating disorders
- phobias
- depression
- alcoholism
- solvent abuse or drug dependency
- mental health problems
- panic attacks
- in debt
- worried about redundancy or retirement
- victim of harassment
- health problems arising from long-term sickness
- accident or trauma victims.

How counselling works
Counselling is only undertaken if an individual feels it would be beneficial and decides to accept the service on offer. Success depends on there being mutual trust and respect between the

parties, and an understanding that everything said is treated as confidential.

The number of counselling sessions necessary can vary from a single session to ongoing contact lasting several months. Counselling takes place within a supportive professional relationship that is non-judgemental, completely safe and allows sensitive issues to be explored without embarrassment or fear that confidential information will feed back to line management.

Counselling allows difficult relationship problems to be explored and the individual time to come to terms with the need to make changes. An action plan can be jointly agreed, building on the trust and confidence that has developed. Hopefully, the personal problems which have been barriers to effective and productive work can be overcome and normal working life quickly resumed.

ADDRESSING HEALTH CONCERNS

Everyone occasionally needs to take time off work because they are genuinely unwell. There are two kinds of sick absence:

- irregular attendance,
- a period of long-term absence.

Irregular attendance

Colleagues sometimes attend irregularly because there is an underlying medical problem which can eventually mean they have to seek medical retirement.

Others have a series of genuine medical absences, which are unrelated. Their irregular attendance needs to be handled sympathetically and sensitively, particularly if the cumulative effect of their sickness is a considerable amount of time off work. In the final analysis, if an improvement cannot be achieved they may have to be medically retired or released on the grounds of inefficiency.

Abusers

The most challenging form of irregular attendance to deal with is the colleague whose absences are not a result of genuine sickness. Those who abuse the system tend to adopt three methods:

- **Liars**. Those who ring in sick when they are perfectly fit and well.

- **Skivers**. Those who make the most of a minor illness, like a cold, and exploit the system by:
  - (a) taking sick leave when other colleagues would come to work
  - (b) taking an inordinate amount of time to recover and return to work.

- **bolshy**. Colleagues who go sick in retaliation for a manager making a decision they dislike, for instance refusing a request for annual leave on operational grounds.

Monitoring absence
Introduce a monitoring system where line managers are:

- responsible for recording all sick absence

- checking whether there is a pattern of absence

- determining the reason for any sick absence.

Sound judgement and common sense are needed when dealing with colleagues who are off work due to sickness. It is important everyone is dealt with fairly and that the genuinely sick colleague is not made to feel a criminal. If the activities of abusers are not checked a conscientious worker has extra work to do. This undermines morale and motivation, particularly if it is common knowledge that the team member is not genuinely incapacitated.

Follow-up action
All suspected abuse shoud be thoroughly investigated. Where high levels of sickness occur, colleagues should be:

- interviewed on their return from sicknes;

- issued with a formal warning if the cumulative level of sickness, over a given period of time, is excessive;

- warned that disciplinary action may be taken if high levels of absence continue.

Taking action
There are several sanctions that can be taken against those who abuse the sick system:

- Stopping pay: colleagues are only entitled to sick pay if they are genuinely unfit for duty.

- Withdrawing the concession of self-certification: every day's absence has to be supported by a doctor's note.

- Dismissal: anyone who has been formally warned for abusing the system can be dismissed.

Dealing with long-term absence

Anyone who is unfit to continue normal working can be retired early on health grounds, providing they:

- are unfit for duty

- have a medical condition which is irreversible.

It is normal for a company to involve the occupational health service adviser and welfare officer in cases where early retirement is being considered. Medical retirement is a sensitive matter and all medical information must be treated as strictly confidential.

HAVING A WINNING ATTITUDE

Nothing succeeds like success. Successful people make things happen, enjoy life to the full and are popular with their colleagues. They achieve their goals and are respected by their boss. Be positive and have complete confidence in your own ability. Consider every problem a challenge, another opportunity to demonstrate your problem-solving ability and prove your value to the business.

Keep yourself highly motivated by keeping interested in your career. Maintain interest in the business by being vigilant and discovering ways to achieve further improvements. Increased job satisfaction is guaranteed because getting results builds self-esteem and self-confidence.

Be proactive and use your initiative. This demonstrates you have good ideas, enthusiasm, self-confidence and leadership qualities. Every new project is an opportunity to promote your case for advancement to your boss.

Reaping the benefits of a winning attitude

Winners have the strength of character to persevere and the determination to succeed. Above all, they are positive and highly motivated. This approach brings the following benefits:

- increased vigour
- an enthusiastic approach
- high energy levels
- the motivation and desire to achieve goals
- a strong commitment to the company
- increased levels of self-confidence
- high self-esteem
- loyalty to the company
- feeling valued as a team member.

A winning formula

Winners are more successful than other colleagues because they work harder at being better than everyone else. They are not always the most highly skilled, but what they lack in skill they make up for in other ways. Winners enjoy greater success because they are more:

- committed
- determined
- enthusiastic
- productive
- hard-working
- energetic
- confident
- skilful
- politically astute.

Having a winning edge

Successful people have a winning edge for two reasons:

- they are committed to a process of continuous **self-improvement**;

- they have well-developed **inter-personal skills**.

Self-improvement

Your positive attitude stems from a desire to maximise your potential and use your talents to the full. Don't settle for being as good as other colleagues; be better!

Inter-personal skills

A vital skill to develop is the ability to get along with other people. Learn the skill of motivating others and cultivate a reputation of being a good team member. Be seen as supportive, loyal and discreet.

Develop the art of managing upwards and work effectively with your colleagues. This is the key to managerial success.

Some final thoughts

The sky is the limit:

- **Anything is possible**. Work hard, believe in yourself, and achieve your goals.

- **Plan for success**. Those who fail to plan are planning to fail.

- **Enjoy your success**. Remember you have earned it.

MAKING A PERSONAL ACTION PLAN

1. Observe the way your boss and colleagues interact.

2. Critically examine how you interact with othe team members.

3. Does the team have members with health care concerns whose attendance is irregular?

4. Identify any instances where you have offered support to a team member who has faced a personal crisis.

5. Consider how you can be more sensitive towards the needs of colleagues.

6. Seek feedback from a colleague and your line manager on your rating as a caring colleague.

Glossary

Accountable. The organisation chart shows the chain of command and describes who individuals are answerable to for performing their duties effectively.

Assertive. Standing up for yourself and believing you deserve respect.

Cognitive skills. A knowledge base that has developed through an ability to understand and process information.

Collaboration. The art of getting people with different interests to work together.

Competency-based model. An approach which identifies the core skills necessary to perform the job effectively.

Counselling. A professional service that enables individuals with personal problems to explore their feelings and come to terms with their difficulties.

Credibility. Behaving in a way that is consistent with the values of the business.

Customer focus. Putting the interests of customers first.

Delegating. Developing the skills of subordinates by allocating work, which is part of your normal duties, to them.

Egotistical. A selfish person who is full of their own self-importance.

Empire builders. Their primary interest is to meet their power needs by manoeuvring to increase the number of resources they manage.

Empowering. Being given the necessary power and authority to do something.

Expertise. Specialist knowledge and skill.

Goals. The method used to achieve the vision for the company.

Integration. The art of getting people in different parts of the company to work together as a cohesive group.

Inter-personal skills. The ability to get along well with other people in the company at all levels.

Job description. A document that lists the main responsibilities and duties of the postholder.

Leadership. The personal qualities and methods a manager uses to motivate, stimulate and inspire the team to work together and achieve the company's goals.

Management style. The way a manager leads their team and uses authority to achieve results. Management styles vary from the autocratic and task orientated, to participative and democratic.

Mentor. A manager who coaches individuals they consider have potential.

Motivation. A leader whose personality and vision energises others to work hard, be productive and be committed to achieving goals.

Negotiations. Discussions between parties with different interests, who are trying to find a mutually satisfying compromise solution.

Networking. The process of making useful business contacts, often through social activities.

Ownership. Commitment which is founded in a strong belief in what the team is involved in doing.

Performance criteria. The methodology used to judge overall performance.

Professional. Someone with specialist skills and training whose behaviour and work is of a consistently high standard.

Self-appraisal. An objective examination of your strengths and weaknesses.

Sexual harassment. A misuse of power and form of bullying where the victim is subjected to behaviour that is embarrassing or aimed at gaining sexual favours.

Shareholders. The owners of a limited company.

Skills audit. A comprehensive assessment of an individual's personal, professional, administrative and managerial skills.

Stereotyping. An assumption based on the mistaken belief that a group of individuals share the same negative traits and characteristics.

Strategy. A plan to achieve the goals of the business.

Task orientated. The sole interest is achieving the company's goals.

Teamwork. Working together to achieve a common goal.

Transactional analysis. An analytical tool which describes the roles people adopt and how they relate to each other.

Transferable skills. A range of generic professional skills, including inter-personal skills, which are in wide demand.

Values. The standard of behaviour that is expected from every-body working for the company.

Vision. The principles, beliefs and value system of the company.

Winning. Highly successful.

Further Reading

How to Manage Your Career, Roger Jones (How To Books, 1996).

Managing Through People, John Humphries (How To Books, 3rd edition, 1998).

Investing in People, Dr Harley Turnbull (How To Books, 1996).

Managing Performance Reviews, Nigel Hunt (How To Books, 4th edition, 1999).

Taking on Staff, David Greenwood (How To Books, 1996).

Managing Your Sales Team, John Humphries (How To Books, 2nd edition, 1999).

Moving into Management, Julie-Ann Amos (How To Books, 2nd edition, 2000).

Useful Addresses

CITIZENS ADVICE BUREAU

National Association of Citizens Advice Bureaux, 115 Pentonville Road, London N1 9LZ. Tel: (020) 7833 2181.

EQUAL OPPORTUNITIES

Equal Opportunities Commission (England), Overseas House, Quay Street, Manchester M3 3HN. Tel: (0161) 833 9244.

Equal Opportunities Commission (Wales), Caerwys House, Windsor Lane, Cardiff CF1 1LB. Tel: (029) 2034 3552.

Equal Opportunities Commission (Scotland), St Andrew House, 141 West Nile Street, Glasgow G1 2RN. Tel: (0141) 332 8018.

Equal Opportunities Commission for Northern Ireland, Chamber of Commerce Street, 22 Great Victoria Street, Belfast BT2 7BA. Tel: (028) 9024 2752.

HEALTH AND SAFETY

Health and Safety Executive Books, PO Box 1999, Sudbury, Suffolk CO10 6FS. Tel: (01787) 881165.

INDUSTRIAL TRIBUNALS

Employment Tribunal Service (Head Office), 19–29 Woburn Place, London WCH 0LU. Tel: (020) 7273 8666.

Employment Tribunal Service (England and Wales), 100 Southgate Street, Bury St Andrews, Suffolk IP33 2AQ. Tel: (0345) 959775.

Employment Service Tribunals (Scotland), Eagle Buildings, 215 Bothwell Street, Glasgow G2 7TS. Tel: (0141) 204 0730.

Industrial and Fair Employment Tribunal, Long Bridge House, 20–25 Waring Street, Belfast BT1 2EB. Tel: (028) 9032 7666.

INVESTORS IN PEOPLE

Investors in People UK, 4th Floor, 7–10 Chandos Street, London W1M 9DE. Tel: (020) 7636 2386.

RACE RELATIONS

Commission for Racial Equality, Elliott House, 10–12 Allington Street, London SW1E 5EH. Tel: (020) 7828 7022.

REHABILITATING OFFENDERS

Apex House, St Alphage House, Wingate Annex, 2 Fore Street, London EC2Y 5DA. Tel: (020) 7638 5931).

SEXUAL HARASSMENT

Women Against Sexual Harassment, 312 The Chandlery, 50 Westminster Bridge Road, London SE1 7QY. Tel: (020) 7721 7592 or 7594.

Index

gm Course Tech

market

Risk

New Design / trend

Enterprise Culture .

matrix

prodi. MKT